D1581433

The life of Jesus as recorded by
MATTHEW,
MARK AND LUKE

In case you think this isn't for you

This is for people who don't read the Bible, or who find its world hard to enter and explore.

It is odd that the Bible is read so little, given that it's the world's best-selling book by quite a margin.

Many imagine that it's boring, untrue and irrelevant – or even repressive: all about rules and regulations designed to stop us enjoying life.

Which again is odd, given that its central character is better known and more admired across the globe today than many others you might care to name.

Those who met Jesus were changed forever by their encounter. People are still meeting him today.

My aim, like those who wrote about Jesus in the Bible, is to introduce you to Jesus, whether for the very first time or in a fresh way. So I've tried to imagine how those authors might have written had they been alive today.

If there's even a possibility that the claims Jesus made are true, I hope you will agree that it's worth exploring them for yourself.

Which bit of the Bible is this?

The fullest accounts of Jesus' life and death are found at the beginning of the New Testament. Called 'Gospels' (meaning 'good news'), they were written by four of his followers: Matthew, Mark, Luke and John.

Their accounts pose the question which seems to have been on the lips of everyone who met Jesus, whether follower or opponent. Who is he?

Like all eyewitnesses, the Gospel writers describe the same events from different viewpoints. Matthew, Mark and Luke set out their material in a very similar way so I've blended their accounts into one single life of Jesus.

So what's it all about?

Jesus invited people into what he called 'God's Kingdom'. Unlike any worldly kingdom, it's made up of those who place their faith in him and seek to follow him. Jesus' original followers believed that his death made it possible for anyone who trusts him to live for ever with God.

Sounds unbelievable? Well, you'll have to make up your own mind, but the original writers all accepted death rather than retract what they believed. They were convinced that what you are about to read is true.

Millions of people around the world have found that the invitation is as fresh today as it ever was.

Background – if you're into that sort of thing

Jesus was a Jew, born at a time when Israel was part of the Roman Empire, which had installed a man named Herod as its puppet king. Jews called people from any other nations 'Gentiles'.

Everyday Jewish life was controlled by a small elite of Jewish priests and teachers. They were divided into two main parties: the Pharisees, who were keen to maintain what they believed to be the purity of Jewish worship and had added countless rules and regulations to the original Law taught by Moses, and the Sadducees, who were proud that they provided the Chief Priests every year even though they had to collaborate with the ruling Roman occupiers.

Some of these religious rulers sought to honour God and serve their people, but many loved to think they were superior to everyone else and a significant number opposed Jesus' message about God's Kingdom from the start. They were the very people who should have welcomed Jesus with open arms, but sadly they were more concerned with their own status and privileged position within society than in seeing God's Kingdom established.

Jesus challenged their whole view of life, with its 'thou shalt not' insistence on rules for rules' sake. Instead, he reminded them of God's compassion and his longing to welcome everyone who wanted to see earth look more like heaven.

You will notice that Jesus regularly found himself on the wrong side of the religious authorities by responding to people's needs rather than observing the rules.

Get stuck into the story!

Paul Langham

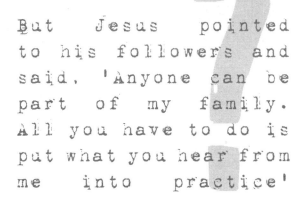

But Jesus pointed to his followers and said, 'Anyone can be part of my family. All you have to do is put what you hear from me into practice'

Dear Reader,

Many of us have attempted to record the extraordinary things we have seen. We have undertaken painstaking research, checking with other eyewitnesses to ensure that what we write is as accurate as possible. We have written it for you, to reassure you that it really did happen.

God promises a Saviour

Hundreds of years before Jesus was born, God had promised his people that he would send a Saviour to our world. This promise was recorded and written down by prophets to whom God revealed the future. The Saviour would be called

Zechariah nearly jumped out of his skin

'Messiah' or 'Christ'. Both words mean 'Chosen One'. Part of the promise was that he would be descended from David, Israel's greatest king, and that's exactly what the family tree of Jesus Christ shows. In fact, his ancestors go right back to Abraham himself.

Our story begins with an elderly Jewish priest named Zechariah. He and his wife Elizabeth were godly people and led blameless lives, obeying God's commandments. The only thing missing from their lives was a child. They would have loved to be parents, but old age had ended that hope.

One day Zechariah was on duty in the temple and people were praying outside as usual. Without warning, an angel appeared in the temple and Zechariah nearly jumped out of his skin.

'Don't be afraid,' said the angel. 'My name is Gabriel and I've come to tell you that God has heard your prayers. Elizabeth is going to have a baby boy and you're to name him John. What a joy he'll be to you – and not just to you. Many people will thank God for him. God will fill him with his Holy Spirit and he will reawaken the faith of many people, preparing them to receive their Saviour.'

Zechariah simply couldn't believe what he was hearing. After all, he knew that what the angel was telling him was humanly impossible.

'As you won't take God at his word,' said Gabriel, 'you won't be able to speak a word of your own until the day your son is born.'

By this time, the people waiting outside the temple were beginning to wonder what had happened to Zechariah. When he came out, unable to speak and using sign language to communicate, they realised he must have seen a vision.

Sure enough, Elizabeth became pregnant. Every day she praised God for blessing her with such an unexpected gift.

Mary and Joseph

About six months later, God sent the same angel to a young woman called Mary, who lived in Nazareth, a town in Galilee. She was engaged to a man named Joseph. They were an ordinary young couple, enjoying all the excitement of planning their future. Seeing the shock and fear on Mary's face, the angel said, 'Don't be afraid, Mary. My name is Gabriel and God has sent me to tell you that he's going to bless you.'

Mary was badly shaken and wondered what on earth the angel could mean. But Gabriel reassured her. 'There's no need to worry, Mary. God is going to give you a baby boy and you must call him Jesus. He will be a great man and will be known as God's Son. God will give him the throne of his ancestor, King David. But unlike David, your son's Kingdom will never end.'

'But how?' Mary asked. 'I'm a virgin.'

Gabriel explained that God's Holy Spirit would form the baby within her. He reminded Mary that Zechariah's wife, one of her own relatives, was now well into her pregnancy. Gabriel encouraged Mary to believe that nothing is impossible with God.

Mary responded with simple, accepting faith. 'I'm honoured to serve God in whatever way he sees fit.'

Some while later, Mary discovered that she was indeed pregnant. What was Joseph to think? *They were an* The only logical conclusion was that she *ordinary young* must have been unfaithful to him. But *couple* he was a caring man and did not want to shame her, so he decided to break off their engagement with minimum fuss.

But that night he had a dream in which an angel told him, 'Don't worry about marrying Mary. She has done nothing wrong. Her pregnancy is unique. The baby boy inside her is created by God himself. Name him Jesus, meaning "Saviour", because he'll save people from their sins.'

What was happening to Mary had been described by one of God's prophets, some eight hundred years earlier:

> *A virgin will have a baby boy and in him God will live*
> *among the people of earth.*

Joseph did as the angel said and married Mary.

Mary visits her cousin

After Gabriel had left, Mary wasted no time in going to see Elizabeth. As soon as Elizabeth heard Mary's voice, her own baby leaped inside her. She was filled with God's Holy Spirit and cried out, 'O Mary, Mary, this is so amazing! You're more highly honoured than any other woman, to be chosen to carry this child. You'll be greatly blessed for taking God at his word and believing that what he told you would come to pass.'

Mary couldn't contain her joy and a spontaneous shout of praise burst from her lips:

> *'How wonderful God is, that my Saviour should*
> *take an interest in someone as ordinary as me!*
> *Future generations will marvel at what God*
> *has done for me.*
>
> *'He's perfect, flawless, and his mercy knows no limits,*
> *embracing everyone who honours him, across the*
> *generations.*
>
> *'No one can match his strength or his mighty acts.*
> *He brings the arrogant down to earth with a bump,*
> *even if they sit on thrones!*
>
> *'But he welcomes with open arms those who think*
> *they're nothing special.*
>
> *'He fills the hungry to bursting, but turns away empty-*
> *handed those who consider themselves rich enough*
> *without him.*
>
> *'He stands by his people and never forgets the promises*
> *he made to our ancestors, right back to Abraham.'*

Mary stayed with Elizabeth for about three months and then returned home.

John the baptiser is born

In due course, Elizabeth gave birth to a son. Her family and friends came to celebrate God's kindness to her. When it came to naming the boy, everyone assumed he would be called Zechariah after his father, but Elizabeth insisted he be called John. This was quite a departure from tradition and they were uncertain what to do. Zechariah was still unable to speak, so they gave him a clay tablet on which he wrote just one word: 'John'. As soon as he had done this, in obedience to what the angel had told him, he found he could speak again. Filled with the Holy Spirit, Zechariah poured out his praise and wonder:

'What an amazing God we have!
Raise the roof with shouts of praise!
He's about to make good on his promises of old.
Watch his salvation plan unfold!

'He's going to pluck us clean out of our enemies' hands
and shower us with mercy,
because he never forgets his promises.
He'll ride to the rescue and sweep away all who hate us,
so that we can live God's way without fear to the end of
*   our days.*

'As for you, my precious son, you will be a mighty
*   messenger of God.*
You will roll out the red carpet for the coming Saviour.
He will unlock the gate of salvation and bring forgiveness
*   to everyone.*

'God's tender love will rise like the sun at dawn,
bringing the night to an end and driving away even
*   death's deep shadows,*
so that we can rediscover the way to live in peace.'

This became the talk of the whole region and there was intense speculation about what would happen when the boy was older.

Jesus is born

At about this time, Caesar Augustus, the Roman Emperor, ordered a census of his entire empire. This required every man to return to his place of birth to register, along with his immediate family.

Joseph, as a descendant of David, went to Bethlehem with Mary, who was heavily pregnant. And that's how Jesus came to be born in Bethlehem. Because of the chaos caused by the census, Mary and Joseph had nowhere to stay except a stable, so Mary wrapped her newborn son up tight and put him to sleep in the animals' feeding trough.

The shepherds and the angels

In the fields around Bethlehem that night, shepherds were guarding their flocks. Without warning, the darkness exploded into blazing light and an angel stood before them. The shepherds were terrified, but the angel said, 'Don't be scared. Listen to me: I bring good news for the whole world! This very night your Saviour – everyone's Saviour – has been born right here in Bethlehem. He'll be easy to find. He'll be the only newborn baby lying in an animal feeding trough.'

Then the sky was full of angels, calling out, 'God's glory is splashed across the skies and his peace has come to earth. Peace to all who find favour with him!'

As suddenly as the angels had appeared, the night sky became empty and still again. The shepherds jumped up, *Without warning, the* left everything and hurried off to *darkness exploded* Bethlehem, where they found the very scene the angel had described: Mary and Joseph in the stable, with their baby lying in a feeding trough.

Mary locked these memories away in her heart and treasured them for the rest of her life.

The shepherds went back to their fields, glorifying and praising God for all the things they had heard and seen, which were just as they had been told. What a story they had to tell – and tell it they did, to everyone who would listen.

Jesus is named and dedicated

When Jesus was eight days old, according to custom, he was circumcised and given the name Jesus, just as the angel had instructed Joseph.

A little while later, again in accordance with their tradition, Joseph and Mary took Jesus to Jerusalem to dedicate him to God.

There was a holy man in Jerusalem called Simeon, who lived God's way with the help of the Holy Spirit. He had spent his life longing for salvation to come to Israel. The Holy Spirit prompted him to go to the temple on the very day Jesus' parents brought him there. Simeon took Jesus in his arms and praised God: 'Lord God, King over all, you have kept your promise and I can now die content, because I have witnessed the unveiling of your salvation plan. This child will shine brightly in the darkness of this world and reveal truth to people across the world and in generations yet to come.'

Mary and Joseph listened in stunned silence. Then Simeon asked for God's blessing on them and said to Mary, Jesus' mother, 'Your child faces a great and terrible destiny. Some *'Your own heart will be torn in two'* people will walk into life through him, others will stumble and fall because they refuse to accept the truth he brings, and some will even turn against him. The secrets of many hearts will be laid bare. And the day will come when your own heart will be torn in two.'

Also in the temple that day was an elderly widow called Anna, who spent her days in the temple worshipping God. As Simeon finished speaking, she began to tell everyone there that this child was God's salvation plan for his people.

The Magi visit Jesus

Sometime after Jesus was born in Bethlehem, men of learning arrived in Israel's capital city, Jerusalem, asking, 'Where's the new king? His star has appeared in the night sky and we have followed it here from our homelands far to the east, so that we can pay him homage.'

When Herod heard this, he was alarmed and began some research of his own, asking the Jewish religious leaders where they believed the Messiah would be born.

'In Bethlehem,' they replied. 'The ancient prophecy is quite explicit:

'Bethlehem, your future conceals a wonderful privilege:
you will produce a ruler to shepherd God's people.'

Herod called the travellers to meet him and persuaded them to tell him when exactly they first saw the star. 'Search in Bethlehem,' he told them. 'Let me know where you find this baby king. You can be sure I'll want to pay him a visit as soon as I can…'

The travellers set off and the star led them to the very place where Jesus and his parents were staying. They were overjoyed when they saw Jesus and gave him lavish gifts which expressed the worship of their hearts. Later, warned in a dream about Herod's true motives, they slipped quietly out of the country without reporting back to him.

King Herod tries to kill Jesus

That night, an angel once again visited Joseph in his dreams. 'Get up. There's no time to lose. You have to get Mary and Jesus out of here, now. Go to Egypt and lie low until I tell you. Herod's going to try to kill your son.'

Again, Joseph followed the angel's instructions to the letter, escaping to Egypt with Mary and Jesus in the nick of time.

'Herod's going to try to kill your son' When Herod realised he'd been tricked, he exploded with rage and ordered his soldiers to kill every little boy aged two and under in Bethlehem and its region. Long ago, the prophet Jeremiah had predicted this:

> *Listen to the voices wailing with the agony of grief,*
> *the screams of mothers refusing to be comforted,*
> *for their sons are all dead.*

Jesus grows up in Nazareth

Eventually Herod died, and Joseph had another dream. 'You can go home now,' the angel said. 'The coast is clear.'

So Joseph took Mary and Jesus back to their own land, where they set up home in Nazareth, just as predicted by one of God's ancient prophets. Jesus grew into a strong young man known for his wisdom.

Each year, Mary and Joseph travelled to Jerusalem for Passover, a national festival celebrating the time long ago when Moses had led their ancestors out of slavery in Egypt to their new homeland.

One year, when Jesus was twelve, they were on their way home from Jerusalem, assuming that Jesus was with other members of the party. That evening they realised he was missing and returned to Jerusalem to look for him. After three frantic days of searching, they found him in the temple among the religious teachers, not just listening, but asking questions and giving answers which astonished everyone who heard him.

'How could you do this to us?' Mary scolded him. 'We've been worried sick about you!'

'Why?' asked Jesus. 'Surely you could have guessed I'd be here, in my Father's house?' But they didn't understand what he meant.

So they returned home and Jesus gave them no more cause for concern, but Mary added this to her store of memories. Jesus grew strong in body and wise in character. God smiled on him and people thought highly of him.

John the baptiser prepares the way for Jesus

Years later, when Tiberius Caesar had been emperor for fifteen years, another Herod was the Romans' puppet ruler in Israel, Pontius Pilate was governor of Judea, and Annas and Caiaphas were Jewish high priests in Israel. God gave John, the son of Zechariah and Elizabeth, a mission. He had grown into a fine young man, strong and godly in character, and for years had lived out in the desert, waiting for his moment to come.

Now John began to preach in the desert, telling everyone who came to listen, 'The time has come to change your hearts and minds. Turn from your selfish ways. God is about to establish his Kingdom on earth in a new way. Start living in a way that pleases him.'

Long ago, Isaiah, one of God's prophets, had predicted:

A voice calling out of the desert, 'Get ready to meet
with God who is coming to deliver his people. Put out
the red carpet to welcome him. Every barrier and obstacle
which prevents people seeing God's saving power must
be removed.'

John's message was simple and effective. He called people to turn to God, and they did, flocking to John from all over the region, from cities and villages alike. As a sign that they acknowledged all the things that were wrong in their lives and were serious about turning back to God, John baptised them in the River Jordan. This earned him the nickname 'John the baptiser'.

But when John saw members of the ruling religious elite coming to find out what was going on, he rounded on them. 'Snakes!' he shouted. 'What are you doing here? Don't think your pedigree is going to save you. "We're OK," you say. "We can do as we please because we're descended from Abraham." Let me tell you, God decides who Abraham's real children are.

You're like a tree that has started producing rotten fruit. Mend your ways, or the axe is going to fall. Trees that don't produce good fruit end up on the bonfire.'

The crowds didn't like the sound of this. 'How can we avoid this fate?' they asked.

'Be generous,' replied John. 'Share what you have with those in need.'

Tax collectors were among his audience. They were universally hated because they worked for the Romans and *'I'm only the warm-up for the main act'* lined their pockets by overcharging their own people. When they asked how they should respond, John told them, 'Only collect what you're supposed to, not a penny more.' To soldiers, John said, 'Don't take people's money by force. Be content with your army pay and don't bring false charges against people.'

John's powerful preaching and uncompromising message made people wonder whether he was the promised Saviour. Expectation hung in the air. But he would have none of it. 'Listen!' he said. 'I'm only the warm-up for the main act. I can put you into water as a symbol of your desire to turn away from sin and start a new life, but I can't give you that new life itself. Look for the Saviour who is on his way. He's so much more important than me that I wouldn't be worthy to lace his shoes. He'll fill everyone who accepts and trusts him with God's Holy Spirit. Like a fire blazing within you, he'll burn off all your impurities and give you fresh energy to live God's way.'

John continued in this vein day after day, encouraging people to respond to God's invitation to new life.

Jesus is baptised

One day, Jesus came to the River Jordan and asked John to baptise him.

'Surely not,' said John. ' It should be the other way round. You have no wrongdoing to confess.'

But Jesus said, 'Do as I ask. If I'm to fulfil my mission, and do it faithfully as a human being, I must be baptised like everyone else.'

As Jesus stepped out of the river, he saw heaven open above him and the Holy Spirit resting on him in the form of a dove. Then God said, 'My Son, I want you to know how much I love you. Everything about you pleases me. You're my heart's delight.'

Jesus was about thirty at this time and was well known as Joseph's son.

Jesus is tempted in the desert

Immediately, the Holy Spirit led Jesus into the desert to face God's Enemy, who wants to ruin every good thing that God has planned.

After forty days without food he was famished and the devil sidled up, tempting him to abandon God's way.

'If you really are God's Son,' the devil mocked, 'why put up with hunger? Surely you could turn this stone into bread and eat your fill?'

Jesus replied, 'Scripture tells me that it's better to have a heart full of God's words than a belly full of bread.'

The next moment, Jesus found himself standing on top of Jerusalem's temple. 'If you really are God's Son, jump!' called Satan. 'Doesn't God's Word promise that he'll send angels to catch you before you hit the ground?'

'Yes it does,' said Jesus. 'But it also warns us not to challenge God to prove himself.'

The tempter then conjured up a vision of all the world's empires and the splendour of human society. 'It's all yours,' he whispered in Jesus' ear. 'All you have to do is bow to me.'

'Get out of here, Satan!' Jesus ordered. 'God's Word tells me to worship him and him alone.'

So the Enemy gave up, for the moment.

Jesus delivers his manifesto

Not long after this, John was arrested and put in prison. Hearing this, Jesus went back to Galilee and settled for a while in the lakeside town of Capernaum, *'God's Kingdom is only* where word of his presence spread. *a heartbeat away'* He was filled with God's Spirit and people listened eagerly to what he had to say. Long ago, the prophet Isaiah had predicted:

> *Our people will experience a new dawn at the end of*
> *a long, dark night. They will step out of death's shadow*
> *into new life.*

Jesus began to teach people about his Father's Kingdom. 'Today's the day. God's Kingdom is only a heartbeat away. Turn away from selfishness and believe my message.'

One Day of Rest, Jesus went to the synagogue in Nazareth, where he had grown up. He was handed the scroll recording the words of Isaiah the prophet. Opening it, Jesus chose this passage:

> *God has filled me with his Spirit for a purpose –*
> *to bring his good news to the poor,*
> *to set the captives free,*
> *to open the eyes of the blind,*
> *to lift the hearts of the oppressed,*
> *and to tell everyone the time has come*
> *to accept God's saving power.*

As he finished reading, the atmosphere inside the synagogue was electric. All eyes were glued to Jesus as he said, 'Those ancient words have been waiting for this very day. Today they come true.'

The people were puzzled. Although they were astounded by his teaching, they couldn't get past the fact that they had known him since he was a boy. Their familiarity stopped them recognising him for who he really was.

'Who does he think he is?' they asked. 'He's only a carpenter's lad, Mary's boy. We know his family. So how come he can teach like this?'

'Prophets are recognised and honoured everywhere, except in their own town,' said Jesus sadly. 'God's prophets have always been spurned at home. Take Elijah and Elisha: some of their greatest miracles benefited foreigners rather than their own people.'

This infuriated his listeners. Grabbing hold of Jesus, they frogmarched him up to the edge of a cliff, hell-bent on throwing him to his death. But Jesus walked straight through them and away. Their lack of faith meant that Jesus found it impossible to do many miracles there, which dismayed him.

Jesus begins to gather his team

One day, the crowds were thronging around Jesus right on the edge of the lake. Two sets of brothers were drawing up their boats after a night's fishing. They were Simon and Andrew, and their partners James and John.

Seeing Simon's fishing boat, Jesus stepped into it and asked Simon to push out a little from the shore, where he sat, teaching the people.

Afterwards, he told Simon to pull out to deeper water and throw out his nets. Simon said, 'Master, we've been out all night and caught nothing. All my experience tells me to call it a day, but as it's you...'

Simon and his men cast their nets, which in a moment were bulging with fish and threatening to break. They called their partners in the other boat to help, but the catch was so big that both boats began to sink. They couldn't believe their eyes. Simon fell to his knees. 'Leave me, Lord,' he said to Jesus. 'I'm not fit to be in your presence. If you knew what my life was like, you wouldn't want me anywhere near you.'

'Don't be afraid,' Jesus replied. 'If you think what you've just seen is remarkable, come with me. I'll help you land a much greater catch.'

The four men left everything and followed him.

Jesus proclaims and demonstrates the Kingdom of God

Jesus travelled throughout the region, telling people the good news that God was offering everyone citizenship in his Kingdom. Wherever he went, sickness and disease were cured. Word spread like wildfire and soon the sick and suffering were being brought to him from all corners. Jesus healed them all, releasing those enslaved by God's Enemy. The crowds flocked to him.

It was as if God himself was there

Jesus and his new followers went into Capernaum's synagogue on the weekly Day of Rest, where Jesus started to teach.

One of those present was a man who had been taken over by an evil spirit. In the middle of the service he suddenly screamed at Jesus, 'Are you here to destroy us? I know you, God's Chosen One.'

'Silence!' commanded Jesus. 'Get out!'

The spirit threw the man to the floor, but left without causing further harm. The people, already impressed by Jesus' teaching which put their usual preachers in the shade, were now stunned. They had never known anyone with the authority to do what Jesus did. It was as if God himself was there.

'Did you see that?' they exclaimed. 'He commands evil spirits and they have no choice but to obey him!' The news spread rapidly across the whole region.

After the synagogue service, Jesus and his followers went to the home of Simon and Andrew. Simon's mother-in-law was sick in bed, but as Jesus took her hand, the fever left her and she got up and looked after them.

As darkness fell that evening, people were still bringing the sick and those tormented by evil spirits to Jesus. The entire population of the town crowded round the house and Jesus healed everyone in need, silencing any evil spirits with a word.

One of God's prophets had predicted that the Messiah would take away disease.

Jesus travels around Galilee teaching and healing

In the quiet hours before dawn the next day, Jesus found a place to be alone and pray. But before long Simon and the others tracked him down. 'What are you doing out here?' they asked. 'The whole town's looking for you.'

The crowds arrived and begged him to stay with them. 'I can't,' he replied. 'I've been sent to tell as many people as I can about God's Kingdom, so I must move on.'

So he and his followers set off, speaking in synagogues all over the region and freeing people from demonic oppression. Jesus both proclaimed and demonstrated that God's Kingdom had come.

In one town, a man covered in leprosy fell at Jesus' feet. 'Lord,' he said, 'I know you can heal me. But will you?'

'Will I?' said Jesus, his heart filling with compassion. 'Of course I will!' Touching the leper, he said, 'Be healed.' No sooner had the words left Jesus' mouth than all trace of the man's disease vanished. 'Don't breathe a word about this to anyone,' said Jesus. 'Go to your Jewish priest and do what the Law of Moses requires. Let him check you over and declare you free of disease. Your healing will send a message to the religious leaders.'

'Don't breathe a word'

But of course the man couldn't stop talking about it to everyone he met. Before long, Jesus couldn't go into towns, such was the clamour for him. Yet even in the countryside the crowds found him, so Jesus got into the habit of regularly slipping away to quiet places to pray.

A few days later, Jesus returned to Capernaum. When word got out, so many people crowded into the house where he was staying that they spilled out onto the street as he spoke. Members of the religious ruling elite had come from all over the country and were watching Jesus like hawks.

The power of God was present to heal the sick. A group of men brought a paralysed friend lying on a stretcher, but they couldn't force a way through the crowds. So they climbed up onto the roof, dug through it and lowered their friend down to Jesus' feet. Visibly moved by their belief and determination, Jesus looked at the paralysed man. 'Son,' he said, 'all your sins are forgiven.'

The religious leaders were incensed by Jesus' words. 'This man just claimed to be God!' they thought to themselves. 'Only God can forgive sins. This is blasphemy!'

Jesus could read every thought in their heads and said, 'I know what you're thinking. Words are cheap. How easy to tell someone their sins are forgiven, which can't be proved one way or the other. Perhaps this will convince you that I have authority to release people *'Son,' he said, 'all your sins are forgiven'* from everything which holds them captive. Watch.' He turned back to the paralysed man. 'Get up,' he said. 'You'll walk home today.' To the crowd's astonishment, the man did just that in front of their very eyes. Everyone was talking at once, trying to take in what they had just seen and praising God for the wonder of it all.

Jesus clashes with the religious leaders

One day, Jesus was walking by the lake, with people hanging on his every word. He spotted one of the hated local tax collectors, a man named Matthew, and called out to him, 'Follow me.' Without a second thought, Matthew got up and joined Jesus.

That evening, Matthew threw a party at his house so Jesus could meet some of his friends. The place was full of tax collectors and others the religious elite wouldn't have touched with a bargepole.

'What on earth's he doing with that riff-raff?' they sniffed.

Overhearing them, Jesus asked, 'What use would be a doctor who avoided the sick and only tended healthy people? And why would God send a Saviour who kept his distance from those who so obviously need saving?

'And don't think you don't need saving: everyone does. But it's hard to save those whose self-satisfaction makes them blind to their need of forgiveness. I can only rescue those who realise they need saving.'

Changing tack, the religious leaders said, 'We've noticed that John the baptiser's followers often go without food as part of their spiritual discipline. So do we, and our followers. So why do you and your followers spend so much time eating and drinking?'

'Because it's the only fitting response to what God is doing all around you,' Jesus replied. 'Can you imagine wedding guests ignoring the food laid on at the reception? Of course not. It's a celebration and everyone tucks in. While I'm here, my followers will celebrate. They'll have plenty of time for sorrow when I'm taken away.

'What God is doing is so new that your old religious framework doesn't work any more. You need a complete change of heart and mind. God's Kingdom is like a brand-new shirt. You don't rip it up in order to patch an old tattered one. Nor do you put fine vintage wine in dirty, used bottles. No, you need brand-new, clean bottles. Your religious system of petty rules and regulations is too small and cramped to host God's Kingdom.'

'Loosen up a little and enjoy what God has given!'

One Day of Rest, some Pharisees spotted Jesus and his followers picking a few ears of corn as they walked through a field. 'Law-breakers!' they shouted. 'Don't you know that's against the rules?'

'Go back to our holy writings,' Jesus told them. 'Find the place where King David took consecrated bread and shared it with his men because they were hungry. So he was a law-breaker too, in your book. Yet God didn't make anything like the fuss you're making. And I'm a greater king than David. And what about your Jewish priests? Don't they technically break your law every time they go to work in the temple on a Day of Rest?

'Don't you see how narrow-minded you've become, and how far you've strayed from God's priorities? Doesn't his Word teach us that "Having mercy on those in need is far more important than getting religious ritual correct"? When he gave us a weekly Day of Rest, he meant it to be a blessing, not all this box-ticking and guilt. You can find rest in my Kingdom. In fact, I'm the one for whom the Day of Rest was created. So loosen up a little and enjoy what God has given!'

Jesus heals a man with a withered hand

On another Day of Rest, a man with a deformed hand was in the synagogue where Jesus was teaching. The religious leaders, far from feeling any compassion for him, saw him as bait, wondering if Jesus would go against their rules and heal him.

Jesus knew just what they were thinking. He had the man stand up and asked the people, 'What best fits the spirit of our Day of Rest, doing good or evil? Giving life or taking it away?' No one dared answer. You could have heard a pin drop as people waited to see what Jesus would do next. Jesus scanned the faces of the religious leaders, distressed at the hardness of heart they revealed. 'If one of your animals fell into a pit on the Day of Rest,' he said, 'would you leave it there? So how can you justify leaving this poor man in need until tomorrow? If you can tend to a dumb animal on the Sabbath, I can surely heal this man.'

You could have heard a pin drop

Turning to him, Jesus said, 'Stretch out your hand.' As he did so, everyone saw that it was whole again. The people rejoiced at the sight, but the religious elite were livid and began to plot Jesus' death from that moment.

Jesus, aware of their intentions, slipped away to an open space, where he was surrounded by crowds who were drawn by his teaching and power to heal. Anyone who needed healing was made well, but Jesus urged them not to reveal his identity. Those plagued by evil spirits were set free, their demons screaming that he was the Son of God as they fled. Jesus commanded them all to be silent. Soon everyone was pressing to try to touch him, because healing power was flowing from him.

Here indeed was the Saviour promised by the prophets of old:

> *See my servant, the One I have chosen, the One I love,*
> *the One who delights me. I'll fill him with my Spirit and*
> *he will bring justice to the nations of the earth.*
>
> *He won't need to argue his case or blow his own trumpet:*
> *you won't hear him drawing attention to himself.*
>
> *He'll be gentle and compassionate with those who are*
> *broken or have lost hope and he won't give up until justice*
> *has triumphed. Nations will place their trust in him.*

Jesus chooses his core team

Jesus would spend whole nights praying to God, his Father. After one such night, Jesus selected twelve of his followers to form his core team. There were two sets of brothers: Simon (whom he later renamed Peter) and Andrew, and James and John, whom he nicknamed 'thunder boys'. Then Philip, Bartholomew, Matthew and Thomas, another James, another Simon and two named Judas, one of whom would later turn traitor.

He called them 'apostles' and set about training them to do what he was doing, giving them authority to teach and to work miracles and to drive evil spirits out of people.

Jesus teaches his followers the values of God's Kingdom

Seeing the size of the crowds, Jesus took his followers up a hillside and began to show them the world through God's eyes.

'Let the values of my Father's Kingdom shape your character,' he told them and went on to explain what he meant.

'God loves those who realise that a place in his Kingdom can't be earned through their own efforts, but only received as his free gift. Throwing yourself on his mercy makes you a perfect fit for his Kingdom.

'God's heart goes out to those who grieve. One day, he's going to wrap his arms around them and wipe away their tears.

'God loves those who don't push themselves forward, but instead trust in him. He has a whole new world waiting for them.

'God loves those who ache for right to triumph over wrong, because he wants the same. One day, they'll be able to watch him straighten everything out.

'God loves those who copy him by being merciful to others. He'll always be merciful to them.

'God loves those who won't let anything rotten take root in their hearts. One day, their eyes will drink in all the wonders of heaven.

'God loves those who try to bring his peace to others. He knows it's one of the hardest things, but it's a quality he seeks in all those who long to be adopted as his children.

'God won't let you down when you're hated because you follow me. He'll be right there with you. In fact, when you're pushed to the margins, taunted and rejected because of your faith in me, that's a red-letter day. Celebrate when it happens, because what God has in store for you makes anything this life can offer pale into insignificance.

'This world has always persecuted my faithful people, including the prophets.'

Jesus went on to say, 'Your lives should make people sit up and take notice, like salt in food or light in darkness. Like salt, make life taste better for others. Don't lose your edge, or you'll make no impact on the world around you. Salt that goes stale is thrown out.

'Brighten people's days by letting God's love shine out of you, so they can see things as they really are. What's the point of light if it's hidden away? Shine with God's love, so people will notice and thank him.

'If you've fallen into the trap of thinking that wealth and possessions are what life's about, beware! You may succeed and end up feeling very pleased with yourself for making it, but it's all an illusion. All you've really done is to wrap yourself in cotton wool and pull it over your own eyes.

'If you've stuffed yourself with this world's goodies while others go hungry, beware! After the feast comes famine.

'If you float carelessly through life, treating it all like one big joke, ignoring the suffering around you, beware! When the dam bursts, your tears will never stop.

'If everyone's always telling you how wonderful you are, beware! Compliments can turn to condemnation in the blink of an eye.'

Jesus continues to teach his followers

'I haven't come to overturn what God has taught you through his Law and his prophets down the ages. I've come to give you the power to put that teaching into practice. As long as this world lasts, God's Word remains true and trustworthy. Don't dismiss it, let alone encourage others to ignore it. Practise living according to God's Word and encourage others to do the same.

'God's Word remains true and trustworthy'

'One thing's for sure: you won't get into God's Kingdom if you settle for what your religious leaders call "righteousness". They're happy if they can convince themselves that they're technically on the right side of the Law, but God sees much deeper than that.

'Take murder as an example. The Law's pretty clear. "Don't murder." Sounds simple, doesn't it? The trouble is, it's easy to feel you're OK because you've never actually killed someone. But God meant that law to go much further. God looks right into the heart and sees the hidden anger there, which can so easily lead on to violence. Every evil act begins with a thought. So losing your temper or cursing someone is like stepping onto a dangerous slope. You never know how quickly or how far you might fall. Rather than pat yourself on the back because you're not technically a murderer, look a little deeper.

'Treat others exactly as you would like them to treat you' Is there anyone you've wronged in any way? Seek them out and put it right. Saying sorry now is a small price to pay to avoid things escalating. If someone's got a watertight legal case against you, it's common sense to settle out of court. If you don't, the judge will throw the book at you.

'You've been told that it's wrong to steal someone else's wife or husband. Never done that? Good for you. But don't think you're in the clear. What about those lustful thoughts for the man or woman next door, or at work? As far as God's concerned, you're already breaking his law.

'I'm deadly serious about this. It's a matter of eternal life and death. Faced with that choice, any price is worth paying to ensure you're not left out in the cold.

'God gave marriage as a beautiful gift to men and women. But the religious leaders have made divorce so easy and one-sided that a man simply has to serve notice on his wife and he can throw her out. God meant marriage to be for life and divorce has to be a last resort. Your casual approach risks making adulterers of you all.

'You've been told to keep your promises. Well and good. But why dress them up by swearing by things you can't control? It doesn't say much for your integrity if you have to make extravagant claims to convince people. Make sure you're known as someone whose word can be trusted. Whether it's 'yes' or 'no', people should know they can rely on what you say.

'Long ago, God restrained people's thirst for revenge by limiting retaliation to what the attacker had done to them: "an eye for an eye" and so on. But I challenge you to drop the idea of retaliation altogether. Even if someone assaults you, don't hit back. If someone steals from you, offer more. If someone forces you to help, do more than they demand. It's never crowded on the extra mile. Hold lightly to the things you possess. Give and lend freely to anyone who asks you for something and don't worry about getting it back. Treat others exactly as you would like them to treat you.

'You've been told to love your neighbour. Over the years,

people have added "and hate your enemy". My challenge to you is to love your enemies, be kind to them and ask God to bless those who persecute you. That's how you show the world that you're God's children. God doesn't have favourites and he doesn't just love the lovely. He gives each day and its blessings to everyone, including the unlovable and the downright ungrateful.

'Anyone can love those who love them back. Where's the achievement in that, or in lending to someone you know will repay the loan? The values of God's *'You have to turn your* Kingdom stand those of the world on *thinking upside down'* their head. Lend without expecting any return. If you copy God by doing this, you show yourself to be his child and will be richly rewarded by him. If he's willing to be your Father, you need to be a chip off the old block, showing mercy to everyone. God is perfect and he challenges you to become like him.

'Pay attention! If you want to live God's way, you have to turn your thinking upside down.'

Jesus teaches his followers about prayer

Jesus said, 'Don't flaunt your good deeds in order to win the favour of the crowds. God won't reward you for that. So don't make a song and dance about helping others in need. That's what hypocrites do, getting an instant kick from people's admiration. But that's nothing compared to what God will give to those who do good secretly. He sees everything and will reward your generosity.

'Don't parade your spirituality for all to see and admire. God can't stand hypocrisy. Don't use prayer to impress people. If you do, your reward stops there. Prayer is an intimate expression of your relationship with God and brings its own reward. And there's no need to rabbit on and on, as if God can be impressed with a mountain of words. Remember that God is a good Father who already knows what you need even before you begin.'

One day, Jesus was praying, watched by his followers. When he finished, they asked him to teach them how to pray. In response, he taught them the key principles of talking to God.

'First, God is your heavenly Father. Remember that and it will colour your whole attitude to prayer, because you can tell your Father anything and everything.

'Next, acknowledge that God is holy and ask him to make

earth begin to look like heaven. That's what it means to pray for his Kingdom to come.

'Then turn to your own needs, which are threefold. You have basic physical needs. Ask him to supply what you actually need, rather than all the things you'd like! You also have the spiritual need of forgiveness. As you ask God to forgive you, that's the time to let go of anything you hold against anyone else for anything they've done to you. You're asking God for a clean slate, so do the same for others. Finally, ask for strength to avoid all the temptations this world has to offer.

'Your willingness to forgive others is the key to being forgiven by God. If you want his forgiveness, you must forgive others, whatever they do against you. How can you expect God to forgive you if you hold grudges and refuse to forgive those who've wronged you?

'Going without food for a time is a healthy spiritual discipline, your physical hunger reminding you of your inner hunger to know God. But again, make sure you don't abuse it to gain human approval. If you go round looking miserable and tell everyone what you're doing, human admiration will be all the reward you get. When you fast, don't let it show. Be content with God's reward.'

Jesus teaches his followers about life's priorities

'Don't put your trust in earthly wealth, because your heart will follow your investments. People love to squirrel treasure away and then spend all their time dreaming of it. The trouble is, *'Treasure in heaven can never be lost'* treasure is so fragile and is easily spoilt or stolen. In the end, it's just another thing to worry about. Invest in the life to come rather than this one. Treasure in heaven can never be lost – and your heart will be safe there too.

'When you light your lamps as dusk falls, you don't put them under bowls, do you? Of course not! You set them where they can light the whole room. It's not much fun being in a house in the dark. Imagine yourself as a house. Are its rooms filled with light, or sunk in shadow? Open your eyes to the reality of what God is doing, and it will be like lighting the lamps in a house at the end of the day. Darkness will be scattered and all will be clear.

'Being able to see clearly is a wonderful thing and blindness is a terrible handicap. It's the same with spiritual sight: if you're spiritually blind, you really are in the dark. Can you see beyond the here and now? Do you recognise the truth of what I'm saying?

'You have to choose between earthly wealth and living for your heavenly Father. You can't do both, any more than you can give your best to two different employers at the same time.

'Making that choice sets you free from the curse of worry. In fact, with God as your Father, you don't need to worry about a thing, whether basics like food and clothing, or even life itself. How much more do you think you're worth to God than the birds of the sky? If he looks after them, how much *'Does worrying make you live longer?'* more will he look after you? What good did worrying ever do for anyone anyway? Does worrying make you live longer, or does it just feel like it?

'And why all the endless fuss over what you wear? Think of the most delicate orchid. Its beauty eclipses that of any fashion model, yet its life is so brief. How much more do you think you're worth to God than flowers? Don't you trust him to look after you? People worry about all sorts of things, but God knows what you need. Live one day at a time, trusting him, and make it your priority to live according to the values of his Kingdom. He'll look after everything else.'

Jesus teaches his followers not to judge others

'Don't you dare pick over other people's faults as if you have the right to pass sentence on them. It's so tempting to write other people off and we do it so easily. But if you're harsh in your judgement of others, that's the way God will treat you. So if you want to avoid *'As you give, so you* being weighed in God's balance *will receive'* and found wanting, don't dare look down your nose at anyone. And if you hope God will forgive you, how can you even consider refusing forgiveness to someone else? Be open-handed with everything you have and in return God will fill your hands to overflowing. As you give, so you will receive.

'Would a blind man follow another one? Of course not, unless he wants to end up in the ditch! Is a pupil superior to her teacher? Of course not. But if pupils learn well, they can grow to be like their teacher.

'How come you have X-ray vision when it comes to other people's faults and yet somehow manage to overlook your own? What would you say if a blind person offered to perform laser surgery to cure your slight squint? You wouldn't let them near you! Concentrate on putting your own life in order before you even think of telling others how to live.

'And don't waste your energy where there's no chance of achieving anything. You'll get nothing but pain for your efforts.'

Jesus teaches his followers about seeking God

'When you pray, be persistent. Imagine an old friend arrives unexpectedly at your house late in the evening. You're out of food, so what do you do? You go to a neighbour and ask for some. But he's already tucked up in bed and tells you to go away! Now you have a choice. You can either go away empty-handed, or ask again. If you persist, your neighbour will probably get up and give you what you need. Now, don't imagine God answers prayer just to be rid of you! No, the point is that he loves us to express the depth of our hunger in prayer.

'God is always willing to be found by an honest seeker'

'So, if you're hungry to know God as your Father, ask him and your prayers will be answered. If you're serious about finding God, all you have to do is look. If you truly want to enter God's Kingdom, all you have to do is knock at the door and I will open it for you. God is always willing to be found by an honest seeker. He's longing to be found and doesn't make it hard.

'Remember, he's your Father. You know what parents are like, how they dote on their children! They love giving them good things. Do you have children? If they ask you for fish, would you serve them a snake? Of course not, even though you're far from perfect. Remember that God is your heavenly Father – and he's perfect. You can trust him to give his Holy Spirit to everyone who asks, and whatever he gives you will be good.

'If you treat others the way you would like to be treated, then you'll be doing everything God asks of his people.'

Jesus teaches his followers about the two roads in life

'There are two roads you can take in life. One is "easy street", so broad and flat and busy you can't miss it. It leads to a glittering archway that seems inviting, but in fact is a dead end – literally. The other is just a winding track, steep and hard in places, leading to a narrow door. Few choose it, but that door opens into everlasting life.

'Don't accept anyone who claims to be sent by God until you've had a good look at the way they live. Does that match up with what they say? You can tell what type a tree is from its fruit. If you have a good tree, it will produce tasty fruit. If the tree's bad, the fruit will be sour too. In just the same way, your behaviour reveals what sort of person you are. The quality of the human heart, whether good or bad, overflows into the way we speak and act.

'Don't rely on the way people talk, or even on what they claim to have done. It's not necessarily those who boast about their faith in God who are really his, but those whose lives bring glory to him. And remember what happens to trees which continually produce bad fruit: sooner or later, they get cut down.

'Don't think I can be fooled. There are those who seem to talk the right talk, using all the jargon. But they won't enter my Kingdom unless they walk the walk as well. On Judgement Day, some will claim miracles as their credentials. "Away with you," will be my reply. "I don't know you."

'There's no point paying me lip service and pretending to be my follower if your fine words make no difference to the way you live. That's like building a house on a beach, with no foundations. The storm tide sweeps in and away goes your house! Who would ever do that? Everyone knows that a building needs strong foundations. Life's the same, and I'm the best foundation anyone can have. My words are bedrock, so make sure you build on them and live by them. They're the perfect foundation for a strong life.'

When Jesus stopped speaking, his followers were silent, awed by the wisdom and authority of his words. They had never heard anything like it before.

Jesus demonstrates the Kingdom in power

Jesus returned to Capernaum, where a Roman officer approached him. 'Lord,' he said, 'one of my servants is paralysed and in great pain.' The *The townspeople begged* centurion had become a friend *Jesus to help him* to the Jewish community, even paying for their synagogue, and so the townspeople begged Jesus to help him.

'I'll come and heal him,' replied Jesus. 'No, Lord,' said the centurion. 'I'm not worthy to have you in my home. And anyway, there's no need. I know authority when I see it. As

27

a soldier, I'm under orders myself and when I give orders to my men, I know they will be obeyed. You have authority over everything, so all you have to do is order this sickness to leave my servant.'

Jesus turned to the crowds and said, 'This man's faith is stronger than any I've found among God's own people. Watch

'Young man, I'm talking to you'

out. On Judgement Day, those with faith like this will be gathered from across the world and welcomed into eternal life. They'll take your places in God's Kingdom if you're not careful, leaving you out in the cold.'

Then Jesus turned back to the centurion. 'What you believe is possible has just happened.'

When he got home, the centurion found his servant restored to complete health.

Soon after this, Jesus visited a town called Nain. As always, people thronged about him. At the town gate they met a funeral procession for a young man, the only son of a widow. When Jesus saw her, his heart went out to her and he said, 'Don't cry.' He went over to the coffin and touched it. The pallbearers stopped and Jesus said, 'Young man, I'm talking to you. Get up.'

The young man sat up and spoke. Jesus reunited him with his mother and the crowds, awestruck, began to praise God. 'A powerful prophet is in our midst! God has come to save us.' The news of what had happened spread like wildfire.

John the baptiser sends a question for Jesus

The news reached John the baptiser, who sent two of his own followers to ask Jesus whether he was indeed the Saviour God had promised.

'Go and tell John what you've seen and heard,' Jesus told them. 'Tell him that those who couldn't walk now dance for joy. Tell him that the blind now gaze at everything that moves. Describe the new baby-soft skin of the lepers, the deaf revelling in birdsong. Tell him the dead draw breath again. Tell him that the good news is proclaimed to the poor. Above all, tell him not to lose faith!'

After John's followers left, Jesus asked the crowds about him. 'What drew you out into the desert? A weakling? No! What then, a celebrity? Of course not, you go to the posh part of town for that! So what drew you to John? You recognised that he was a messenger from God. In fact, he's as important a prophet as God has ever sent, the very one promised in the ancient prophecies:

I'll send my messenger to announce the arrival of the Saviour.

'No one in all human history is as significant as John. Yet the least member of God's Kingdom is greater! The Kingdom is spreading and you need great resolve to enter it. Believe me when I say that John is the one whose coming heralds the Saviour.'

Turning to the religious leaders, Jesus said, 'Your generation has been given the privilege of seeing all this happen, but you're blind and deaf to the reality of what God is doing in your midst. You're like a group of toddlers in the playground, constantly dissatisfied, always wanting something else. "We put on party music, but you wouldn't dance," you whine. "So we played a lament, and you shed no tears."

'John lived a life of self-denial and you said he was possessed. I come and share your lifestyle and you condemn me as a glutton and a drunkard! I can't win. You complain that I spend time with people you consider beyond the pale.

'Still, those who are wise can see the truth and time will tell against you. Had previous generations seen the miracles you've seen, they would have repented in a flash, as would some foreign cities I could *'You're like a group of toddlers in the playground'* mention. How much worse it will be for you than for them on God's Judgement Day.'

Jesus then prayed, 'Thank you, Father, King of creation, for revealing the secret of your Kingdom to ordinary people, while those who pride themselves on their intellect struggle to get their heads round it.'

Jesus then told them, 'My Father has brought me into his confidence. I'm the only one who truly knows him. And the only way anyone else can meet him is if I make the introduction.'

Then Jesus turned to the crowds. 'Are you weighed down with the burdens of life?' he asked. 'Is it all just too much of a struggle? What a relief it would be to find someone to help you through it! I'm that someone. Come to me and let me soothe your soul. Following me is easy compared with struggling to live life in your own strength.'

After this, Jesus resumed his travels, telling people about the good news of God's love wherever he went. The twelve members of his core team travelled with him, along with a number of women who supported his ministry out of their own means.

Jesus clashes again with the religious leaders

On another occasion, Jesus healed a man tormented by an evil spirit which had robbed him of speech and sight. Seeing this, the crowds were amazed. 'Surely,' they said, 'this can't be anyone other than the Saviour!'

But the Pharisees repeated their earlier accusation. 'He's in league with God's Enemy. That's how he does it!'

Jesus couldn't believe what he was hearing. 'How can I be freeing people from the Enemy's power if I'm working with him?' he shot back. 'Why would any general fight against his own troops? And if what you're saying were true, how do you explain your own exorcisms? I'll tell you what's really going on here. This world is like a community living in terror of the neighbourhood bully. You've become so used to Satan throwing his weight around that you think he's too strong to resist. Well, I've come to take him on and I'm winning hands down. He's a thug who has stolen lives and I'm here to set them free.

'So choose your side, because the world's at war and in this battle between good and evil, you're either for me or against me. Be very careful before you deliberately mess with *'The world's at war'* the boundaries between God and his Enemy. God's offer of forgiveness is total and absolute. He's able and willing to forgive anything you do or say, even if it's against me. But if you start calling good evil and evil good, you're on a slippery slope. You risk becoming so hard-hearted that you lose any sensitivity to right and wrong and before long you won't be able or willing to ask for forgiveness.

'Don't think that you can say what you like without consequence. Words matter: like fruit on a tree, they reveal the state of your heart, whether good or bad. So be careful with your words. God is listening. On Judgement Day, every careless word will be broadcast. Your words will determine whether you are charged or acquitted.'

Some of the religious leaders called out, 'Put on a show for us! Do a miracle.'

'Your very request shows your lack of faith in God,' Jesus replied. 'There's only one sign coming your way. Do you remember Jonah? He spent three days inside a huge fish. In the same way, I will spend three days inside the earth. That's the only sign you're going to get. Work it out if you can. The people Jonah was sent to call to repentance will put you to shame on Judgement Day, because they listened to his message and mended their ways. And Jonah's a little fish compared to me.

'The Queen of Sheba travelled the world to hear Solomon's wisdom. Her example puts you to shame, because you have God's own Son speaking to you and still you won't listen.

'Beware of the spiritual vacuum which characterises this generation. Don't think it's enough for the owner of the house simply to evict the squatter, splash a fresh coat of paint on and put everything back where it was. What's to stop the squatter coming back and this time bringing his gang with him? Imagine the state of the house then! When I drive out demons, you need to fill the space left with the presence of God. Blessed are those who hear my teaching and follow it.'

Jesus invites everyone to join his family

Then someone called out, 'Jesus, your mother and brothers are outside. They want to talk to you.'

But Jesus pointed to his followers and said, 'Anyone can be part of my family. All you have to do is put what you hear from me into practice.'

Jesus uses stories with hidden meaning to teach the people

Later that day, Jesus left the house and sat by the lake. So many people crowded round that he had to speak to them from a boat on the lake while they stood on the shore. He began to tell them parables – stories with hidden meanings about the Kingdom of God.

The story of the sower

'Imagine a farmer walking across his land, a bag of seed around his neck. As he walks, he picks up the rhythm of sowing, scattering the seed from side to side. Where it falls determines its fate.

'On the pathway, trodden hard by countless feet, the birds have a field day. The seed that falls there is gobbled up fast.

'Some falls among rocks, where the soil is shallow. Plants

shoot up and seem to thrive at first, but the roots have no depth and the sun soon kills them off.

'Where the ground is full of weeds and thorns, the young plants don't stand a chance. They're throttled at birth.

'But some seed falls into rich, deep soil. Up it grows, strong and healthy, producing an abundant crop out of all proportion to the tiny seed from which it grew. Do you get the message? If you do, pay attention to it!'

Later, on their own with Jesus, his followers asked him, 'Why do you speak in stories?'

'It's a way of testing people,' he replied. 'The key to the stories lies in the hearts of the listeners. Each story contains a message about God's Kingdom, like jam in a doughnut. Those who only nibble at the outside never find it, but those with real hunger find an explosion of taste just when they least expect it.

'Those who are just looking to be entertained by the latest novelty preacher simply hear the stories, but can't fathom their meaning. Those who truly want to find God pick up on the message they tell.

'An ancient prophet summed up this generation when he wrote:

> *You'll hear every word, but understand nothing,*
> *see every detail, but miss the big picture,*
> *because your hearts are hard and callous.*
> *So your hearing and sight grow weak,*
> *preventing you from acknowledging your need of healing.*

'Some people can't see the wood for the trees, while others don't let my words past their ears. What a privilege God has given you, not only to see and hear, but to understand these things. You have no idea how many generations have longed to experience this.

'Take the story of the farmer and the seed. That's an easy one! Can't you see? The farmer is God and the seed is his invitation to life which he scatters everywhere.

'The different soils represent the people who hear the good news I'm bringing about God's love, and the fate of the seed says something about their different responses to my message.

'Some people's hearts have been trodden rock hard. The message never penetrates the surface and it's easy for the Enemy to snatch the message away from them almost before they realise what's happening.

'Some people make an instant but shallow response. At first they seem to thrive, but there's no depth to their commitment or understanding and when the heat's on and life gets a little tough, they fade away.

'Others want to accept God's invitation, but their lives are overgrown with distractions. The message has no chance to ripen and mature before the cares of this world throttle their good intentions.

'Then there are those whose lives are ready for the good news. Like seed falling into rich and freshly turned soil, the good news goes deep and takes root in heart and mind, producing *'Put a little trust in me'* a huge harvest out of all proportion to the tiny seed from which it grew. Such people go from strength to strength. Their transformation is amazing.

'The good news of God's Kingdom is like a spotlight, showing up what's in the dark corners of people's lives. When the lights are on, there's nowhere to hide. You can't keep secrets from God. He sees into the deepest shadows and one day he's going to lay everything open to public view.

'So weigh my words carefully. Your response to God's invitation is crucial. Be generous and open-handed in all your dealings, and he will give you life. Put a little trust in me, and God will multiply your investment. Be tight-fisted, and you'll lose out. Trusting yourself is like keeping all your money under the mattress: you're likely to lose the lot.'

The story of the wheat and the weeds

Then Jesus turned back to the crowd. 'Imagine another farmer. He prepares his field for planting and then sows wheat. While he's asleep that night, an enemy slips into the field and sows a load of weeds out of sheer spite. Sure enough, when the plants begin to come up, the farmer finds his field full of both wheat and weeds. What's he going to do? Try to pull out all the weeds without damaging the wheat? Not a chance. He waits until harvest time and then sorts it out. He stores away the wheat safe and sound in his barns, but he flings the weeds on the bonfire.'

The story of the harvest

'Imagine another farmer. Once he has sown his seed, the rest is up to God. The crop grows all by itself. The farmer can neither make it happen nor explain how it happens. He has little more to do until harvest time. The power for growth is in the seed itself, and so it is with the good news of God's Kingdom.'

The story of the mustard seed and the yeast

'Imagine a mustard seed, the smallest there is. Looking at it, you'd never guess that it would grow into a tree that can shelter a whole flock of birds. But that's what happens, and so it is with God's Kingdom. It might not seem much to write home about at the moment, but it will grow big enough to shelter everyone who runs for its cover.

'Or think of yeast. You only need a tiny amount mixed with dough to make bread rise.'

Jesus explains the stories

Jesus used these word-pictures to reveal different aspects of the truth about God's Kingdom. The ancient prophets had foretold that the Saviour would speak in stories:

> *I'll use stories to unlock secrets hidden since the dawn of time.*

Every time Jesus spoke to the crowds, he used stories like these. He only explained their meanings to his followers.

When they were alone again, his followers asked Jesus to explain the story of the wheat and the weeds.

'I'm the farmer, and the field is planet earth,' he explained. 'In this story, the wheat represents those who accept my Father's invitation to enter his Kingdom. The weeds represent those whom the Enemy entices to turn against God. The harvest is the end of the world. So take warning from what happens to the weeds. They're rooted out and burned. At the end of time, the angels will root out everything and everyone who spoils this life. But those who accept God's Kingdom will bask in his love for ever.'

The story of the hidden treasure

'Imagine a jeweller who finds the biggest diamond in the world, buried in someone else's field. He's so excited that he'll do anything, anything at all, to get his hands on that field, even if it means selling everything else he owns. Knowing God is worth far, far more than any fortune, so make sure you don't miss out. It's the greatest treasure in the whole world.'

The story of the fishing net

'Imagine a fishing trawler, far out at sea. Its net pulls up all sorts of fish, but there's no way to sort them until the boat's back in harbour. Only then can the fishermen sort out the good from the bad. The good fish are stored safe and sound. The bad ones are thrown away. That's how it will be on Judgement Day. The angels will separate out those who have put their trust in me from those who haven't.

'Do you get it yet?' Jesus asked his followers.

'Yes,' they answered.

Jesus calms a storm

As the crowds grew larger, Jesus and his followers left by boat for the other side of Lake Galilee. One of its infamous sudden storms blew in and the waves threatened to engulf the boat. Jesus, exhausted by *'Who is this man?'* all he had done that day, had gone to sleep. His followers began to panic and shook him awake.

'Save us!' they screamed. 'We're all going to drown!'

'Why are you so afraid? Don't you trust me?' said Jesus. Standing up, he simply told the wind and waves to stop and the storm died away in an instant.

His followers were stunned, unable to grasp fully what they had just seen. 'Who is this man?' they whispered to one another. 'It's as if nature were a pet dog which he can bring to heel with a single command.'

Jesus frees a man from the torment of an evil spirit

When they arrived on the far side of the lake, they met a man who had been tormented by demons for many years. He roamed the area naked and lived in a graveyard. The locals had tried restraining him, but even chains couldn't hold him, so they now kept well clear. His cries echoed around the hills day and night and his body was a mess of self-inflicted wounds.

'You're not wanted here, Son of the almighty God!' he screamed.

'Get out!' Jesus commanded. The man collapsed, writhing at Jesus' feet, and screamed at the top of his voice, 'Why have you come here? Please don't torture me!'

'Give me your name,' demanded Jesus.

'Legion,' the demon replied, 'because there are many of us. You can't touch us before Judgement Day. But if you're going to send us away, send us into that herd of pigs over there.'

Jesus gave them leave and the evil spirits fled to the pigs. The entire herd, about two thousand pigs in all, went berserk, rushed over a cliff into the lake and drowned.

The pig herders ran for their lives and news of what had *People ran from all* happened spread quickly. People ran *directions* from all directions to see what had caused the commotion. When they saw the man calm, dressed and as sane as anyone else, fear rippled through the crowd and they begged Jesus to leave.

The man pleaded to go with Jesus, but he gently told him to stay. 'Go home,' he said, 'and tell people what God has done for you.'

He did just that, setting that whole area buzzing with his story.

Jesus heals an old woman and raises a young girl from the dead

No sooner had Jesus returned to the other side of the lake, than the crowds surged around him again. One of the leaders of the local synagogue, a man named Jairus, fought his way through, fell at Jesus' feet and begged him for help. 'Come to my house, please. My little girl, my precious only child, is dying.'

Jesus agreed and they set off, but the crowd was so large that it became almost impossible to make headway. As Jesus and his followers were pushing their way through, a woman struggled towards them. She had suffered from continual bleeding for twelve long years, despite going to doctor after doctor. Their ineffective treatment had cost her every penny she had and she was desperate.

'This is my chance,' she thought. 'If I can only touch him, I'll be healed.'

Approaching Jesus from behind so as not to be seen, she pushed her hand through the tangle of bodies pressing around him and grabbed his cloak. Sure enough, she felt her body mend as she stood there and knew that her years of suffering were over. The bleeding had stopped.

Jesus felt a surge of power leave him. Stopping in his tracks, he scanned the faces in the crowd and called out, 'Who touched my cloak?'

His disciples were staggered. 'The crowd's wild,' they replied. 'Can't you see them pressing around you? It would be easier to ask who didn't touch you!'

But Jesus kept looking from face to face, until the woman, realising she was found out, came forward, fearing that he would be angry with her. Falling to her knees before him, she poured out the whole story.

'My dear child,' Jesus said, 'God has responded to your faith. You are well: no more suffering for you. Go in peace.'

While all this was happening, some friends of Jairus arrived and broke the news that his daughter had died. 'There's no point Jesus coming now,' they said.

'The girl's not dead, just sleeping'

Ignoring them, Jesus looked Jairus straight in the eye. 'Don't abandon hope,' he said. 'Trust me, and all will be well.'

When they arrived at the house, they found it in uproar, full of mourners weeping and wailing. 'Out, all of you!' commanded Jesus. 'The girl's not dead, just sleeping.'

They laughed in his face, but he turned them out, leaving only the girl's parents to stay in the room, along with Peter, James and John.

'Get up, little one,' Jesus said, taking the girl by the hand. She sat up, got out of bed and walked round the room. Her parents were overcome with joy. Jesus told them to give her something to eat and urged them not to tell anyone what had happened.

But news spread quickly.

Jesus sends out his team to do what he has been doing

As Jesus travelled from town to town, teaching and healing people, his heart broke for the crowds who flocked to him. They were so lost and helpless, like sheep without a shepherd to lead them and keep them safe.

'See the state of the world,' he said to his team. 'It's like a field at harvest time. So many men and women are just waiting to accept God's invitation to life, but who will deliver that invitation? Ask God for more people to join us in this work.'

Jesus then commissioned his twelve closest followers to go out in pairs and do all the things they had seen him do. He gave them authority to drive evil spirits from people and to heal them.

He gave them precise instructions. 'Focus on the lost sheep among our own people, the Jews. Proclaim this simple message: "God's Kingdom is coming." Demonstrate this by healing the sick, bringing the dead back to life, making lepers whole and casting out evil spirits. Be as generous to others as

God has been to you. Travel light: the only thing you need is a staff for walking. Nothing else, no cash, no food, no bag, no change of clothes. Accept food and lodging wherever you find it.

'Wherever you go, find somewhere to stay and ask God to bless those who are willing to welcome you. But don't waste your time in any place where the people aren't interested to hear what you have to say. Simply move on to the next place, but warn them that they're making a dangerous mistake. Those who reject you will be sorry come Judgement Day.

'You're like children being sent out among wild animals. Be savvy to the ways of the world without letting it pollute you. Don't expect a warm welcome. You'll face hatred and even violence because you follow me. You'll be arrested and hauled up in front of the authorities to explain your actions. In that way you'll become my witnesses to Jews and Gentiles alike. When they arrest you, don't be anxious about what to say. When the time comes, God's Spirit himself will inspire your words.

'My coming to earth means war, and following me will test even the closest loyalties to breaking point: families will be split down the middle as people choose for or against me. Your devotion to me must come above all other loyalties.

'You'll draw the world's hatred and never be able to settle long anywhere. You'll always be at risk of persecution and death. Keep going, no matter what, and you'll be safe in the end. I will be revealed before you've completed your mission.

'Students model themselves on their teacher and his reputation becomes theirs. If people call me the devil, how much more will they accuse you?

'Ideas are to the mind what yeast is to bread. A little yeast can shape a whole loaf. So beware of the religious leaders' teaching. Don't fear them or let their teaching shape the way you think, because God will one day bring everything out into the open and you'll be vindicated. There'll be no shadows in which to hide. Things you have whispered in secret will be broadcast from the rooftops. So proclaim publicly the things I've told you privately.

'Keep going, no matter what, and you'll be safe in the end'

'Don't fear death, or those who deal in it, because this earthly life pales into insignificance compared with eternity. And the only one who can give you eternal life is God himself, so you do well to pay far more attention to him than anyone else. But you don't need to cower before him. Trust him, because he already values people far more than anything else he created. Birds are ten a penny, but he watches over them. How much more will he take care of you? Why, he even knows how many hairs you have on your head! But beware of the Enemy, who can destroy your soul.

'To welcome me is to welcome God himself'

'Acknowledge me now, and I will welcome you when I return to earth at the end of time with my angel armies. Disown me now, and that welcome will be withdrawn. Speaking against me is one thing. That can be forgiven. But if you begin to distort the work of the Holy Spirit, if you begin to call "light" "darkness", then you're in danger of placing yourself outside the reach of God's forgiveness.

'Anyone who welcomes you welcomes me, and to welcome me is to welcome God himself. All who welcome him will be rewarded. The smallest act of kindness shown to my followers will not go unnoticed.'

John the baptiser is executed

Jesus then moved on to the towns of Galilee. The twelve set off, calling people to acknowledge their sins and turn to God for forgiveness. They commanded evil spirits to leave their victims and anointed the sick with oil. All were healed.

Israel was now ruled by another Roman puppet king, named Herod after his father, the king who had tried to kill Jesus as a baby. Herod had thrown John the baptiser into prison because John had publicly denounced him for living with a woman called Herodias, who was his own brother's wife. Herod nursed his grudge against John, but kept him alive because the people held John in high esteem. Deep down, Herod envied John's inner strength and goodness, which only increased the king's hatred and fear. He found John's teaching fascinating and yet baffling.

Herod's birthday came and he threw a lavish party for all the important people of the land. The highlight of the evening was a dance by Herodias's daughter, who delighted the assembled guests so much that Herod rashly promised her whatever she wanted. Her mother, seeing her opportunity for revenge, told her to ask for John the baptiser's head, served up on a tray. Herod was mortified, but rather than lose face before his guests, he gave the order. John was executed that same hour and the girl gave his severed head to her mother.

When John's followers learned of this, they took his body away and buried it, and sent word to Jesus. On hearing the news of his cousin's death, Jesus slipped away to be alone.

Jesus feeds thousands of people

Jesus' followers returned from their mission, eager to tell him all that had happened. They tried to go by boat to a quieter spot, but the crowd followed along the shore. More and more people joined the chase, so when Jesus and his friends landed, they found thousands of people already waiting.

'Are you joking?' they asked

Jesus' heart went out to them. He explained about God's Kingdom and healed the sick, until the evening drew in and his followers began to fret about food.

'It's getting late and there's nothing to eat out here,' they said. 'Shouldn't you send the people home?'

'Why don't you give them something to eat?' Jesus replied.

'Are you joking?' they asked. 'It would take almost a year's wages to buy enough food for all these people!'

'Well, what have you got?' asked Jesus.

They rummaged round and came up with five bread rolls and a few fish.

'Bring them to me,' said Jesus. Then he asked them to sit all the people down in groups of fifty or a hundred. He took the rolls and fish and, looking up to heaven, thanked God for the food and broke it into pieces. He passed the pieces to his followers, who in turn passed them on to the people. The food kept on coming, until the entire crowd, numbering more than five thousand, had eaten their fill. Afterwards, Jesus' followers gathered up the leftovers in twelve large baskets.

As soon as the people were fed, Jesus packed his followers into the boat, telling them to sail to a town called Bethsaida while he sent the people home. Then he walked alone into the hills to pray.

Jesus walks on water

Night fell and another of Lake Galilee's sudden storms blew up. Jesus looked out to where his followers were struggling to make headway against the wind, pulling on their oars for all they were worth.

At about three in the morning, he went out to them, walking on the surface of the lake. As he drew nearer, he made as if to walk straight past them, but they saw him. Clinging to the pitching boat, they screamed in terror, 'It's a ghost!'

But Jesus said, 'Don't panic, it's only me.'

'If it's really you,' Peter called out, 'let me walk on water too.'

'Come on, then,' Jesus said.

So Peter clambered over the side of the boat and took a few steps towards Jesus. But then he looked around at the waves and began to sink. 'Save me!' he shouted.

They screamed in terror, 'It's a ghost!'

Jesus seized his hand and held him. 'You would have been fine if only you'd kept your eyes on me,' he said.

As they got into the boat, the storm died away and all was calm again. His followers had no more doubts about who Jesus was. 'Now we know you're the Son of God,' they said.

They dropped anchor on the other side of the lake. Even at that early hour, word spread that Jesus had arrived. Wherever he went throughout the region, a steady stream of sick people came to him, begging just to touch the hem of his cloak. All who touched him were made well.

More opposition from the religious leaders

The religious authorities continued to snoop around Jesus. Cleanliness was a major feature of their way of life: they had numerous regulations about ceremonial washing before eating. One group came up from Jerusalem and saw Jesus' followers tucking into a meal without going through the rituals they deemed essential.

'We can't help but notice that your people disdain the traditions of our ancestors,' they sniffed.

'You hypocrites!' cried Jesus. 'Talk about double standards! You have abandoned God's commands and are clinging to your own traditions. What a dreadful exchange you've made, and all to enable you to evade God's requirements for holy living. You claim to revere Moses, who taught you to honour your parents. Yet you sidestep responsibility for your parents by claiming that the money they need in their old age is going to God instead. And that's just one example of your contempt for God and his Word.

'The prophets summed you up long ago:

'Your faith is barely skin deep:
you're full of fine talk, but your hearts are cold.

Your attempts to please me are all in vain,
because you have replaced my life-giving Law with
burdensome rules you dreamed up yourselves.'

Turning to the crowd, Jesus said, 'Listen to me. Don't swallow their line that being clean and pure in God's sight is a matter of external rituals and rules. God sees beneath the skin, beyond appearances, into all the things which make us morally unclean. It's our inner life God is concerned to set right – our hearts and minds, the way we think, the way we treat people. That's what counts to him. It's what comes out of your mouth that defiles you, not what goes in.'

'The Pharisees don't like being contradicted,' his followers warned him.

'Those so-called religious "leaders" had better watch out,' Jesus replied. 'Remember the story of the wheat and the weeds. Anyone not planted by my Father will be pulled up by the roots. Pay no attention to them. They're about as much use as a blind guide. Anyone who follows them is going to end up in a ditch.'

'I don't understand,' said Peter. 'What did you mean about what comes out of our mouths defiling us?'

'How can you be so slow?' asked Jesus. 'Don't you see that what goes into your body can't pollute you? Food simply passes through. Spiritual and moral cleanliness is all to do with your heart and mind. What comes out of them makes a lasting impression, whether for good or ill. It's the quality of your inner life that counts, because everything which spoils human life comes from within, whether murder or immorality, theft or slander. Being clean or dirty on the outside is neither here nor there as far as God's concerned.'

Jesus heals a woman's daughter

Jesus moved on to the coast, in the vicinity of Tyre. Try as he might, he couldn't keep his whereabouts secret. As soon as she heard the rumours of his presence, a Greek woman came and begged him, 'Son of the great King David, take pity on me. My daughter is tormented by an evil spirit.'

Jesus remained silent, wanting to discern her faith, but his followers couldn't wait to be rid of her. 'Tell her to get lost,' they urged him. 'What a racket she's making!'

'My mission was only to my own people,' Jesus said.

At this the woman threw herself down at Jesus' feet. 'Help

me!' she begged.

'How can I take food meant for children and throw it to animals?' Jesus asked.

'You don't need to,' she replied, 'because no one minds if the animals eat what the children drop.'

Her response was all Jesus needed. 'What faith you have!' he cried. 'What persistence! Go. You'll find your daughter quite well.'

When she got home, her daughter was sleeping peacefully. The evil spirit had gone.

Jesus heals a man who could neither hear nor speak

Jesus moved on again and stayed for a while in the region known as 'the ten towns'. Sick people came in great numbers and many of them had to be carried by friends or family. Jesus healed them all. The crowds praised God for what Jesus was doing.

One day, a man who could neither hear nor speak was brought to him. Sensing that the crowd was more interested in a performance than in the man himself, *Jesus healed them all* Jesus took him aside. He placed his fingers in the man's ears and touched his tongue. Looking up to heaven, he sighed deeply and said, 'Be unblocked.' As he spoke, the man found he could both hear and speak clearly.

Jesus commanded the people not to tell a soul, but the more he insisted, the more they blurted out the news. How could they contain what they had seen and heard? 'Is there anything this man can't do?' people wondered. 'He even cures those who can neither hear nor speak.'

Jesus multiplies food again

After three days of teaching and healing the crowds, Jesus called his followers. 'My heart goes out to these people,' he said. 'They've been here for three days without food. They need to eat, or they'll never make it home.'

'There's no way we could find enough bread in such a remote place,' they told him.

'What have you got?' Jesus asked.

'Seven loaves,' they replied. 'And a few fish.'

As he had done only a few days before, Jesus sat the people down and gave thanks to God. He then broke the food for his followers to pass out among them. This time, over four thousand people ate until they could eat no more, and again the leftovers filled several baskets.

The religious leaders demand proof from Jesus

The Pharisees and Sadducees came to Jesus and asked him to perform a 'sign from heaven' for them, to prove his credentials.

'How extraordinary,' Jesus replied. 'You know how to read the sky: "Red sky at night, shepherd's delight; red sky in the morning, shepherd's warning." Yet you have no idea what God is doing. And you're supposed to be the spiritual leaders of these people? I've already told you. Look for the sign of Jonah. It's the only one you'll get.' With those words, Jesus left them.

'All your religious teachers can give you is religious junk food'

Jesus and his team set out to cross the lake. Once under way, Jesus told them, 'Watch out for the yeast of your so-called religious leaders.'

His followers tried to work out what he meant. 'He's telling us off for not bringing any bread with us,' they murmured.

'Are you still in the dark?' Jesus asked. 'Remember that twice now I've fed thousands with just a small amount of food. When will the penny drop that I'm not talking about physical food? Remember that a small amount of yeast spreads through the whole loaf. That's fine if the yeast is good, but if it's bad, it ruins everything. I can satisfy your spiritual hunger. All your religious teachers can give you is religious junk food.'

Then his followers understood that he was warning them against the teaching of the religious elite.

Jesus heals a blind man

Jesus and his followers arrived in a village called Bethsaida, where some people pleaded with Jesus to heal a blind friend. Jesus took the man outside the village, spat on his eyes and placed his hands on him. 'Can you see anything?' he asked.

The man peered about. 'I think I can see people, but they're all blurred.'

Jesus touched his eyes again and this time he could see clearly. Jesus then told him to go straight home without entering the village again.

Jesus asks life's key question

When Herod heard about Jesus and the wonders he did, he was sure that John the baptiser had come back from the dead to haunt him and was eager to see Jesus in action.

Jesus asked his followers what people were saying about him. 'All sorts of theories are peddled,' they told him. 'Some say you're one of God's prophets come back to life. Others claim you're John the baptiser.'

'Listen,' he replied. 'This is life's key question. Who do you think I am?'

Before the others could speak, Peter said, 'You are the Messiah, the Chosen One, the Saviour of the world.'

'Well done, Peter,' said Jesus. 'God himself has revealed this to you. Your name means "rock", and as you and others proclaim this truth about me, it will become the foundation for the Church I will build on it. Hell itself will be powerless to resist *'Who do you think I am?'* you. I'll give you the keys to my Father's Kingdom. See what my Father is doing, and then work with him to accomplish it here on earth. But don't breathe a word about who I am to anyone.'

Jesus predicts his death

Knowing they had grasped this truth, Jesus began to explain that he must go to Jerusalem, where he would be put to death by the religious authorities, only for God to raise him to life after three days.

Peter was horrified and pulled Jesus away from the others. 'I won't let that happen,' he swore.

'Oh, Peter,' Jesus said. 'Now I hear the Enemy talking, not my Father. You're doing the Enemy's work if you try to turn me aside from the path my Father has shown me. Don't rely on human logic, but see things through God's eyes.

'That goes for all of you,' said Jesus, turning to the people. 'If you want to follow me, this is the path. No more selfish ambition, no more living life your way. You must be ready and willing to give up your life – but it will be more than worth it. So kill off your *'Those who are willing to stake everything on me will hit the jackpot'* old life, hoist your cross onto your shoulders day by day and follow me. I'm going to my death and you must be willing to suffer too.

'If you want to find true life, you must be willing to stake everything on me and my message. Then you'll find a life rich beyond your wildest dreams. Those who set out to guard what they have will lose the lot. But those who are willing to stake everything on me will hit the jackpot.

'Don't sell your soul for a good time. Nothing is more valuable than your soul and nothing in the world is worth the risk of losing out on eternal life. Would you seriously spend a lifetime gathering all the world's wealth, only to find at the end that you've lost the one thing that truly matters?

'I'm giving you fair warning. If you're too embarrassed to admit being my follower, why should I recognise you as mine when I return in glory with all God's angels? Listen: many of you will still be alive when you see God's Kingdom burst on the world in power.'

Jesus is revealed as the Son of God

A few days later, Jesus took Peter, James and John up into the hills. He began to shimmer with light, becoming brighter and brighter until looking at him was like looking at the sun and they had to turn their eyes away.

They became aware that two other figures had joined Jesus and recognised two giants of Jewish history, Moses the law-giver and Elijah the great prophet.

'This is my beloved Son, the apple of my eye'

The three spoke together about Jesus' forthcoming death in Jerusalem.

As Moses and Elijah began to fade, Peter blurted out, 'This is incredible! Why don't I build some shelters so that we can stay here? We need never go back down...' The words were tumbling out of his mouth without him really knowing what he was saying.

As he spoke, they were enveloped in bright cloud and they heard a voice. 'This is my beloved Son, the apple of my eye. Make sure you listen to him.'

At the sound of the voice, they collapsed, terrified. The next thing they knew, Jesus was putting a calming hand on them. 'You can get up now,' he said. 'There's no need to be afraid.'

They looked around, but there was no one except Jesus with them. As they walked down the hill, Jesus warned them, 'What has just happened needs to remain between us until I've been raised from the dead.'

'But our religious instructors teach that the great prophet Elijah must appear to the people before the Saviour arrives,' they said.

'They're right,' replied Jesus. 'But he has already come and gone. They just didn't realise who he was and killed him, just as they will me before long.'

Then they realised he was talking about John the baptiser.

Jesus heals a boy of epilepsy

When they came down from the mountain, they found their friends surrounded by a large crowd, gathered around a man who shouted to Jesus, 'Teacher, please will you help my son? He's my only child and a demon is tormenting him. He suffers convulsions, foams at the mouth and screams with terror. I can't let him out of my sight, because if he collapses into fire or water, I'm terrified he'll die. I begged your followers to cure him, but they couldn't.'

'Give me strength!' Jesus groaned. 'How long must I endure your lack of faith? Bring the boy here.'

When the evil spirit saw Jesus, it convulsed the boy and threw him to the ground, where he rolled around, foaming at the mouth.

'Please,' cried the father, 'if you can do anything to help, have mercy on us and do it!'

'If?' asked Jesus. 'Everything is possible to those with faith.'

'I do believe!' cried the father. 'Help me conquer my doubts.'

Seeing that a crowd was running towards them, Jesus commanded the spirit to leave the boy and never return. With a shriek and a violent convulsion, the *'Help me conquer* spirit left. The boy lay so still that the *my doubts'* crowd thought he was dead, but Jesus pulled him to his feet and reunited him with his father.

Those who saw it were amazed.

Later, his followers asked Jesus, 'Why couldn't we heal the boy?'

'Because your faith is almost non-existent,' Jesus replied. 'Why, if your faith was even the size of a mustard seed, you would be able to move mountains! Nothing would be beyond you. But you need to rely on God's power, not on your own strength. Pray for that power.'

Jesus again predicts his death

While the crowd's attention was taken with all that happened, Jesus turned to his followers and said, 'I will be betrayed and killed – but look to my rising on the third day.'

This filled them with grief, even though they could hardly take it in and were too afraid to question him about it.

Jesus and the temple tax

In one of the local towns, Peter was challenged by some of the temple officials. 'Does Jesus pay the temple tax?'

'Of course he does,' Peter answered.

When Peter returned to the house, Jesus asked him a question. 'When kings raise taxes, do they tax their own children?'

'No,' replied Peter. 'They tax other people.'

'So the children are exempt,' Jesus said. 'But we don't want to get on the wrong side of the law. So go fishing and open the mouth of the first fish you catch. You'll find just the exact number of coins to settle our temple tax.'

Jesus' followers argue about which of them is the greatest

Arriving back in Capernaum one evening, Jesus asked his followers what they had been arguing about on the day's journey. None of them liked to admit that they had been discussing which one of them would be the most important in God's Kingdom.

Jesus gathered the twelve around him and said, 'Let me explain how it works. If you want to be top dog, you must learn to be the servant of everyone else.' Taking a little child in his arms, he said, 'Aren't children wonderful? They trust so simply and so fully. That sort of faith is the key to unlock God's Kingdom.

'Welcome this child, and you welcome me'

'Your thinking must be turned upside down. Want to be important? Position yourself at the bottom of the heap. Want to be greatest? Become the least important of the group. The greatest in God's Kingdom will be whoever has humbled themselves most on earth.

'Welcome this child, and you welcome me. Welcome me, and you welcome God himself. But it would be better to be wrapped in chains and thrown into the sea than to corrupt one of these little ones who trusts in me.'

A man casting out demons

John said, 'There was a man the other day using your name to cast out demons. We soon put a stop to that, because he wasn't one of us!'

'Wrong decision,' said Jesus. 'Anyone who hasn't declared against us is an ally. In fact, if someone so much as gives you water because you belong to me, they will be rewarded.'

Jesus teaches that the way we live has consequences

'Don't fall for the line that it doesn't matter how you live, or that sin doesn't have consequences. Bad things happen in this life and we can't avoid them, but the consequences for those who make them happen are eternal.

'Do anything, anything at all, to make sure you don't miss out on God's Kingdom. If you were trapped in a house on fire, you would do anything to get out, even if it meant chopping off your own foot, losing a hand or gouging out an eye. At least you would live. So when it comes to eternal life, how much more determined should you be? Limp or crawl or grope your way blindly into God's Kingdom if you must. Just make sure you're in. The alternative is to be left out in the cold, separated from God for ever.

'Don't look down on anyone. God sees everything and he has sent me to rescue those who are lost.'

Jesus teaches his followers about reconciliation

'If a fellow believer wrongs you, try to sort it out privately between the two of you. Only if that doesn't work should you involve others, and then only one or two (after all, that's what the Law of Moses advises). If that doesn't put things right, you must tell the church. If he still refuses to repent, he must be disciplined and treated like any other sinner.'

Jesus teaches his followers that they have authority

'I have given you authority. Discern what God is doing in the unseen, heavenly realm, and then act on that here on earth. What God has prohibited there, you must oppose here. What he sets free, you should work to free as well.

'The power of God is present when you meet together and you can ask anything of him if you ask according to my will. Even if there are only a handful of you, I will be there with you.'

Jesus teaches his followers about forgiveness

Peter asked Jesus, 'How many times should I forgive a fellow believer who wrongs me? Seven times, perhaps? Surely that would far exceed any reasonable expectation?'

'Multiply that by seventy, and you might start to get an idea of what forgiveness is really all about,' replied Jesus.

'Imagine a king who calls all his servants to settle their accounts with him,' he continued. 'One of them is in debt to the king for millions, far more than he can ever hope to repay. The king orders the servant's family to be sold. What can the servant do? Falling on his knees, he begs the king to give him another chance to pay – and the king lets him off the whole debt, just like that. But here's the rub. That same servant, as he leaves the king's presence, free from his debt, bumps into a fellow servant who owes him a few pounds. The first servant demands repayment, or else. The second servant does just what the first servant did with the king: he begs for mercy. But the first refuses and has him thrown into prison! When the king hears of this, he's outraged and throws the unforgiving servant into prison. So when you think about forgiving others, remember how much God has forgiven you. How can God show mercy to those who withhold it from someone else?'

Jesus leaves Galilee for Jerusalem

From this moment, knowing that his life was nearing its end, Jesus set his face for Jerusalem. He sent some of his followers ahead to arrange for him to stay in a Samaritan village. Now Samaritans and Jews hated each other in those days and the people of the village refused him entry, because he was heading for Jerusalem.

When James and John learned of this, they went to Jesus. 'Do you want us to destroy them? Let's wipe them out!'

Jesus turned on them, horrified. 'Don't ever think like that again!' he said.

The cost and the joy of following Jesus

As they travelled along, they were met by one of the law teachers. 'I'll follow you to the ends of the earth,' he said to Jesus.

'If you do, you'll be poorer than the birds and beasts,' Jesus warned him. 'At least they have their nests and burrows. But *'You need to decide what's truly important'* those who follow me will have nowhere in this world to call home.'

Jesus called another man to follow him, but the man came up with an excuse. 'Once I've buried my parents and settled their affairs, I'll be free to come.'

Jesus told him, 'You need to decide what's truly important. Anyone can arrange a funeral! I need people who can tell others about God's Kingdom.'

Another man was about to join Jesus when he suddenly got cold feet. Turning away, he called over his shoulder, 'I'll catch you up! I'm just going to say goodbye to my family.'

Jesus said, 'Once you set out to plough a furrow, you can't take your eyes off the line you must follow. In the same way, it's no good being half-hearted about God's Kingdom.'

Jesus sends out a mission team

Jesus chose seventy-two of his followers to go ahead of him in pairs to prepare all the towns and villages on his route. 'There's a huge harvest of lives out there, but so few to bring it in. Ask God for more workers. On your way! This is dangerous work. You'll be like lambs circled by a pack of wolves. Travel light and don't be distracted by idle chit-chat along the way.

'When you go into a house, ask God to bless it with peace. You'll know in your heart whether the owner is for God or against him. Wherever you go, accept whatever hospitality is offered. You're working for the King, so you deserve to be taken care of.

'Your mission is both to proclaim and to demonstrate the Kingdom. Heal the sick and tell everyone that God's Kingdom is close at hand. Not every place will welcome you. When that happens, *'This is dangerous work'* go to the main street and brush the dust off your feet as a sign of their rejection. But even there, you must still give them the message: "God's Kingdom has come near." I can assure you, that town will wish it had acted differently when Judgement Day comes.

'Think of all the towns that have already rejected the good news. Compare them to the most wicked places in history. I tell you straight, if the miracles I've done had been seen in those places, they would have repented and turned to me in a flash. Judgement Day will look more kindly on them than on those who reject me now.

'If people respond to your message, they're responding to me. If they reject it, they reject me. Worse, they reject my Father who sent me.'

The seventy-two returned from their mission full of excitement. 'Using your name, we were even able to drive out demons!' they told Jesus.

Jesus replied, 'I had a vision of Satan plummeting to earth like lightning. I've given you authority to trample evil under your feet and power to overcome anything the Enemy throws at you. But make sure you keep your perspective. It's wonderful to have authority over demons, but even more wonderful that your places in heaven are guaranteed.'

Then Jesus, filled with the Holy Spirit, prayed, 'Father God, you're doing the most amazing things. Those who pride themselves on their intellect just don't realise this, whereas infants in faith can see what's happening. No one can discover or earn your favour through the power of their intellect, but you reveal yourself to people through me.'

Turning to his followers, he said, 'I hope you realise just how privileged you are to be alive at this moment, to see the things you have seen. Generations of people, including kings and prophets, have longed to see and hear the things you're witnessing.'

The story of the good Samaritan

One of the religious experts asked Jesus a testing question. 'How can I make sure of eternal life?'

Jesus asked him a question in return. 'You know the Law. What does that tell you?'

The man replied, 'It teaches me two key principles. First, to love God more than anything else, with every single fibre of my being, and then to love my neighbour just as much as I love myself.'

'That's a great answer,' Jesus said. 'I couldn't have put it better myself.'

But the man was keen to limit the scope of what he had just said, and so he asked, 'The trouble is, who should I regard as my neighbour?' So Jesus told him one of his stories.

'Imagine a man on a business trip. His journey takes him down a country road, where he's set upon by bandits who mug him and steal everything he has, including his clothes. Off they ride, leaving him to die.

'How can I make sure of eternal life?'

'After a while, a Jewish priest comes along. Does he stop to help? No! Maybe he thinks the man's already dead. Maybe he worries that if he touches a corpse, he'll be considered ceremonially unclean and won't be able to work in the temple for a while. Whatever the reason, he hurries past, taking care to avoid contact with the poor victim.

'Still later, the same thing happens again! Along comes a temple assistant, and he hurries by. Maybe he's scared that the bandits will come for him if he hangs around. Maybe his reasons are the same as the first Jewish priest's. Whatever, ritual or fear overcomes any sense of compassion.

'The next traveller to arrive on the scene is a Samaritan.

You would have expected better from our own people than from a foreigner, right? Well, you'd be wrong. Because when he sees the victim, his heart goes out to him. He binds up the man's wounds, sets him on his own donkey and gets him to the nearest inn as quickly as possible. Even though he has to continue his own journey the next day, he leaves enough money with the owner to ensure that the other man is cared for until he returns.

'So, which of the three travellers acted like a true neighbour?'

The religious expert answered, 'The one who showed mercy.'

'There's your answer, then,' said Jesus. 'As far as God is concerned, every human being is our neighbour, whether or not we know or even like them.'

Jesus visits Mary and Martha

At one of the villages on the way to Jerusalem, Jesus and his followers were offered hospitality by two sisters, Martha and Mary. As the evening wore on, Martha found herself becoming irritated with her sister, who, rather than helping her *'Only one thing is truly important'* prepare the rooms and cook the meal, sat spellbound at Jesus' feet as he talked about God's Kingdom.

Finally she'd had enough and said to Jesus, 'Can't you see what's going on? Here I am, doing everything, while Mary's had her feet up all evening. Tell her to lend a hand.'

'Calm yourself, Martha,' Jesus replied. 'Don't let things get on top of you like that. Only one thing is truly important, and that's our relationship with God. Your head's so full of everything that has to be done that there's no space left for him. I can hardly tell Mary off for getting her priorities right.'

Jesus clashes again with the religious leaders

After this, one of the Pharisees invited Jesus to supper and was surprised when Jesus didn't bother with the rules about ceremonial washing before eating.

Reading his mind, Jesus said, 'What's the point of washing the outside of a bowl if you leave the inside filthy? Just so, ceremonial washing is utterly pointless if a person's inner life is corrupt. How crazy to imagine that God, who made and knows your inner life as well as your body, would be fooled for a moment! Put your inner life in order, clean it thoroughly, and then everything else will fall into place.

'Don't imagine for a moment that, just because you stick to the letter of the Law, you can get away with ignoring its spirit. You can tick all the boxes, yet you ignore the foundation principles of the Law – justice and showing the love of God. Focus on the big picture, but don't ignore the little things either.

'Don't you religious grandees just love the best seats in the synagogue? You lap it up when the ordinary people bow and scrape to you! You're like a beautifully manicured lawn laid over a hidden cemetery: perfect on the surface, but rotten deep down.'

Another guest, one of the religious teachers, said, 'Steady on! Don't tar us with the same brush.'

'As for you,' Jesus retorted, 'you should be using your expertise in the holy writings to encourage and inspire the people. You should be lifting their faces to see the God who loves them. Instead, you've become Bible-thumpers, using the Scriptures as a whip to beat the people. You load them with man-made rules. No one can live up to your expectations, so you leave the people crushed under a weight of condemnation. You're so busy wagging your finger at them that you never think to lift a finger to help!

'Focus on the big picture'

'Down the generations, God sent prophets to teach his people – and your ancestors persecuted and killed them! Now you're building elaborate tombs for those same prophets as if that can somehow put things right. All it does is implicate you. So your generation will be held responsible for their crimes as well.

'God wants everyone to enter his Kingdom, but you've lost the key. In blundering about outside, all you're doing is making it harder for anyone else to get in.'

Well, that was some supper party! From that time on, Jesus was a marked man. The religious bigwigs set their faces in opposition to him and besieged him with questions and challenges, hoping to find some way of tripping him up.

The story of the rich fool

One day, someone called out to Jesus, 'Can you settle a family dispute? My brother won't give me my share of our inheritance.'

'Sorry,' said Jesus. 'That's not my place. But I can give you some free advice. Don't let yourself become a prisoner to greed and bitterness. Don't allow your life to be defined by what you have rather than who you are.

'Imagine a wealthy farmer. One year, his land produces a

bumper crop, far more than his barns can store. What to do? "Easy," he thinks. "I'll pull down my barns and build bigger ones. Then I'll pat myself on the back, pour myself a large glass of wine and put my feet up. I've got it made!"

'But God takes a different view. What if the man dies that same night? He has spent his life accumulating wealth he's never going to enjoy, while neglecting the one thing of true significance – his relationship with God. And now it's too late. What a waste! And what a warning to everyone else who thinks that wealth is the thing that counts…'

Jesus teaches his followers to hold the things of this world lightly

Later Jesus told his followers, 'The key to contentment in life is to hold all these things lightly. Don't make material things your main concern. There's more to life than what you can consume, far more. Look at the birds. Do they build barns? No, but God feeds them just the same. And you're infinitely more valuable to God. So stop worrying. Nobody ever gains from worrying. It can't change anything.'

'Picture a lily. Such beauty. Even King Solomon's legendary splendour pales by comparison. If God goes to such extraordinary lengths to create the *'Don't make* beauty of the lily, whose life is over *material things* before you know it, how much more will he look after you? Don't you trust him? *your main concern'* People rush around, frantically trying to find security in things which don't last. Don't be like that. Make God's Kingdom your priority. Then you will have maximum security, and God will take care of everything else.

'You don't even have to worry about finding your way into the Kingdom, because God has gift-wrapped it for you. So unburden yourself of the trappings of this life. Meet the needs of the poor. Nothing in this life lasts in any case. Are any of your investments ever really secure? When you have earthly wealth, you're bound to worry about it. But if you make God's Kingdom your priority, you'll be investing in eternity and you'll have treasure safe from theft and decay. And as your heart always follows your treasure, you'll be safe too.

'John the baptiser told you that I would baptise you with fire, both to burn up what's wrong inside you and to give you power to live. How I long for that fire to sweep through the earth! But I face trials of my own first, before I can complete my mission.

'You know that a cloud coming from the west means rain, and that a southerly wind brings heat. I tell you, storm clouds are gathering. If you can predict the weather, how come you can't read the signs of the times yourselves?

'Imagine you're caught up in a legal dispute. Far better to settle out of court than risk the judgement going against you. Make your peace with God now rather than leaving it to the last minute when it might be too late.'

Jesus responds to a question about natural disasters

Some members of the crowd asked Jesus about victims of natural disasters and the Roman occupation. Did their fate mean they had sinned particularly badly?

'No,' Jesus replied. 'Everyone is equally in need of forgiveness. No one can claim to be better than anyone else. Everyone needs to turn away from sin if they're to find eternal life.

'Imagine a man who planted a fig tree in his vineyard. Three years go by without the tree producing so much as a single fig. So the owner tells his gardener to cut it down. But the gardener persuades him to give it another chance. "Let me work on it," he says. "I'll see if I can help. If not, we'll cut it down next year." God is patient, but he won't wait for ever.'

Jesus heals a woman on a Day of Rest

On one Day of Rest, Jesus was teaching in a synagogue. There was a woman there who had been crippled by a demon for eighteen years. Her body was so bent and twisted that she couldn't stand up straight. Jesus called her forward and told her, 'I release you from this infirmity.' As he placed his hands on her, the people watched her body straighten before their eyes. The woman shouted out her praise to God.

But the man in charge of the synagogue said to the crowd, 'That's enough of that! There are plenty of days in the week for being healed without disrupting the Day of Rest.'

Jesus rounded on him. 'You so-called religious leaders are just a bunch of hypocrites,' he said. 'You don't leave your animals tied up on the Day of Rest. You untie them and let them drink, don't you? How blind can you be? If you're willing to bend the rules for an animal, how can you deny this woman, one of your own people, release from Satan's grip, just because it's the Day of Rest?'

This stinging rebuke made the religious leaders squirm, but the people were overjoyed with what they saw.

Jesus teaches the people about salvation

Jesus continued his journey to Jerusalem, teaching in the towns and villages along the way. Someone asked, 'Is salvation restricted to a favoured few?'

'The door is narrow,' said Jesus. 'You have to let go of all the things you cling to in this life in order to slip through. Many people will try to push their way through, but won't make it. And the door won't be open for ever. A day will come when God will close the door and no matter how hard people beat upon it, it won't open again.

'It won't count for anything that you were aware of me, or even that you associated with me. That won't save you. You'll be left out in the cold and the dark. People from every corner of the globe will be streaming into the party. There'll be nothing you can do. You'll have an eternity to regret your folly in not accepting God's invitation when you were offered it. Some you would think had no chance will be included, and some you would consider cast-iron certainties will be excluded.'

Jesus weeps over Jerusalem

Some Pharisees tried to deflect Jesus from his goal with threats. 'Run,' they told him. 'King Herod is after your blood!'

But Jesus would not be deterred. 'You can give Herod a message from me if you like,' he said. 'Tell him that I'm going to continue my Father's mission, driving *'King Herod is after* out demons and healing the sick right *your blood!'* up to the gates of Jerusalem. Surely you know that Jerusalem is the only place for a prophet to die?

'Oh Jerusalem! Jerusalem!' he lamented. 'They call you "City of Peace", but you've witnessed the rejection and death of God's prophets down the ages. How many times have I tried to gather your people like a hen protecting her chicks under her wings? But each time they push me away, denying themselves the protection they so desperately need. So now you lie undefended, prey to any marauding enemy. Your ruin is just around the corner, although your people will welcome me in through your gates one last time.'

Jesus has dinner with a chief Pharisee

One Day of Rest, Jesus was eating in the house of one of the chief religious leaders. Every eye in the place was on him. One of his fellow guests suffered from painful swellings and

Jesus asked the gathering, 'Can it really be against the Law to heal someone on the Day of Rest?' They didn't respond, so he healed the man before their eyes.

He pressed them further. 'Suppose one of you has an animal which falls into a well on the Day of Rest. Do you leave it there? Or do you pull it out?' But they had no answer.

Seeing how the guests jostled for the best seats at the meal, Jesus warned them, 'Imagine you go to a wedding reception and take a seat at the top table next to the bride and groom. How embarrassing it will be when you're asked to move! Much better to take a lowly place first and then be invited to move to a better seat. If anyone's going to push you forward, let it be God.'

Then Jesus said to his host, 'Next time you throw a party, don't just invite your family, friends and wealthy neighbours. *'Imagine a king who has planned a fabulous banquet to celebrate his son's wedding'* That's fine if you're looking simply for a return invitation or a pat on the back from them. No. Invite those on the margins, the homeless, the addicts, those you normally don't even see. They can't offer you anything in return. But on Judgement Day, God himself will welcome you into the party for the righteous.'

One of the guests pricked up his ears at this. 'Ah, that's more like it! The feast of God's Kingdom. Can't wait!'

'Don't be so confident of your place,' warned Jesus. 'Imagine a king who has planned a fabulous banquet to celebrate his son's wedding. Just the sort of party you're dreaming about. The invitations were sent out weeks before and so, when the great day arrives, the king sends his servants to fetch the invited guests.

'But all the servants get for their trouble is excuses. "I've just sealed a property deal, sorry ... I've got some new cattle to settle in, maybe some other time ... Actually, I've just got married myself, got my mind on other things..."

'Even when he sends more servants to tell them that the food's on the table and getting cold, they refuse to come. Not only do they shun the king's invitation, they kill the very servants sent to call them to the party. Enraged at these insults, the king orders his army to wipe them out.

'Then he tells his servants, "The feast is ready, but we have no guests. Go out into the streets. Bring in the homeless, the blind and the crippled to take the places of those who refused to come." But there's still plenty of room at the party, so the king sends more servants out into the countryside. "Invite anyone you find," he tells them. "Compel people to come in. All those originally invited will miss out."

'But later, the king spots someone not dressed up for the occasion. "How did you get in dressed like that?" he demands. The man has no answer, so the king orders, "Throw him out in the cold."

'God's Kingdom is like a party. He has sent out invitations, but those who were first invited have snubbed their noses at him. So now he's flinging wide the doors to everyone. But take care: when you go to a party, you dress up and look *'God's Kingdom is like a party'* your best. Just so, you need to be sure that your lives please God if you're to stay and enjoy the feast. Otherwise, you'll be shown the door.'

Jesus teaches his followers about the cost of following him

Jesus, wanting to test the enormous crowds who were following him towards Jerusalem, turned to them and said, 'You need to be realistic about the cost of following me. I must come first, ahead of even your love for family. You'll be living on death row as you carry your own cross day by day.' Everyone listening knew that the Romans made death-row prisoners carry their own cross on their way to execution.

'Imagine you decided to build a tower. You don't even begin to dig the foundations until you've worked out whether you can afford to complete the project, do you? Think how ridiculous you would look if you have to stop when all you've done is dig a great big hole!

'Or imagine a king facing war with another king. Before he commits any troops to battle, he's going to get some intelligence about the other king's forces. If he learns that the other king has double his own number of troops, he's going to think twice before going ahead. Surely he'll sue for peace instead? So when it comes to following me, count the cost before signing up. It will cost you everything.

Can you decipher the message in my words?'

The story of the lost sheep

Jesus spent a lot of his time with people the religious leaders wouldn't even acknowledge in the street, such as tax collectors and prostitutes. This confirmed their worst suspicions about him.

So Jesus told them some stories.

'Imagine a farmer who owns a hundred sheep and finds one of them is missing. What does he do? He leaves the others and goes off to find it, of course. He won't stop looking until he finds it and when he does, he's more pleased to see that one sheep than those left safe behind. He carries it home, safe and sound on his shoulders, and calls all his neighbours round to celebrate. In the same way, God longs to seek out all who are lost and bring them home. And let me tell you, heaven celebrates with the return of each one.'

The story of the lost coin

'Imagine a woman who loses a coin. She's got nine others, but that's not the point. She lights a lamp and brushes all her floors until she finds it. Then she calls her friends and neighbours to tell them the good news. "Come on over," she says, "and help me celebrate." God throws a party for the angels every time a sinner turns around and comes home.'

The story of the lost son

'Imagine a father who has two sons. One day, the younger one says, "Dad, I'm fed up waiting for you to die! I need some money now. I want to live a little, see the world. Can you give me my inheritance now?"

'As soon as he gets his hands on the money, the younger son travels abroad and has a wild old time, spending like *"I want to live a little, see the world"* there's no tomorrow. But of course there is a tomorrow, and with it comes cold reality. A famine strikes his new country and he has nothing left to ride it out. Soon he's reduced to scavenging from bins, eating whatever he can find. Even then, he's always hungry.

'Finally he comes to his senses. "This is crazy," he thinks to himself. "My father's labourers live better than this. I'm going home. And when I get there, I'll say, 'Listen, Dad, I know I've blown it. I've been an idiot. I've let you down. I've let God down. I'm not asking for anything except to be taken on as one of your workforce.'" So off he goes.

'How little he knows his father! Since his younger son left, the father has spent each evening roaming the edges of the family estate, straining his eyes into the distance, hoping against hope to see a familiar figure coming home. And one night, it happens! The father can hardly believe his eyes, but as soon as he realises it really is his lost son, his heart leaps, he abandons any sense of dignity and he runs. He runs right up to his son, throws his arms around him and hugs him tight.

'The son begins his speech, which he has been carefully rehearsing all the way home. "Listen, Dad, I know I've blown it. I've been an idiot. I've let you down. I've let God down. I'm not asking for anything except to be taken on as one of your workforce."

'But his father isn't really listening. He's so excited at his son's return that he's already shouting for the servants. "You there! Fetch my best robe. We can't leave my son looking like some vagabond. And you! Quickly now, get the ring he left behind, and his sandals. Just look at the boy's feet! Quickly, now! Tell chef to start cooking. We're going to party all night long! I feared my son was dead, lost to me for ever. And now here he is, safe and sound!"

"We're going to party all night long!"

'But not everyone's happy. The older brother, at work in the fields, hears the music start up and asks one of the servants what's going on. "That brother of yours has finally come home," the servant tells him. "And your father's over the moon about it. There's going to be some party tonight!"

'At this, the older brother goes into a sulk and stays outside, all by himself. When the father hears, he comes and pleads with him to join the celebration. But he says, "I can't believe you're doing this! I've slaved away for you all these years, doing everything you told me, and did you ever once throw me a party like this? Never! But along comes your squalid little son – I won't call him 'brother'! – the one who has whored away your money, and you behave as if it's the best thing that's ever happened to you!"

'"Son," says the father, "I've never denied you anything you've wanted. I've lavished all I have on you. You think throwing a party for your brother is inappropriate? Let me tell you, it's the only proper thing to do! Your brother was as good as dead. It's as though he has come back to life! How can we not celebrate that?"'

The story of the crooked steward

Jesus said to his followers, 'Imagine a wealthy landowner, who learns that his steward has been mismanaging his estate. He calls in the man and demands an explanation. When none is forthcoming, he sacks the steward and tells him to bring the accounts up to date for his successor.

'The manager thinks to himself, "What can I do? I've no chance of finding another job without a reference. I'm not up to labouring and there's no way I'm going to beg on the streets. But hang on! Perhaps I can secure a few favours before I leave…"

'So he summons all his master's tenants to pay their rent. The first one owes £800. "Let's call it £400," says the steward. One after the other, he reduces each tenant's rent.

'The master soon realises what has happened, but what can he do? He can hardly go to all his tenants and demand the original sum! All he can do is grin and bear it. "Clever," he mutters to himself. "Got to hand it to him. Very clever."

'Note that his master didn't commend his dishonesty, but his foresight, his shrewdness in looking to the future. So often, the people who don't know me could teach you a thing or two about planning for the future. If they can do that with earthly things, why can't you do it with regard to your eternal future?

'It's common to give people a little responsibility to start with. How they measure up – whether they show integrity or dishonesty – will give a good guide as to how they can be trusted with greater responsibility. If you can't be trusted to handle this world's wealth, how will you be trusted with eternal riches?

Jesus warns against love of money

'It's impossible for anyone to be wholly loyal to two different masters. You can't be wholly committed to both God and money.'

The religious leaders, who loved money, sneered at these words.

'You spend all your time trying to keep up appearances,' Jesus retorted. 'But my Father sees right through you. He has little time for the things you value so highly.

'Imagine a rich man living in the lap of luxury, his body *'You spend all your* covered in the softest fabrics. Just *time trying to keep* outside his gate lies a beggar, named *up appearances'* Lazarus, his body covered in sores. The garbage from the rich man's kitchen seems like a treat to him.

'Both men die, at which point their fortunes are reversed. The beggar enters paradise, where he joins the great fathers of the faith such as Abraham. The rich man goes to hell, where he endures torment day after day. Looking up, he spies Abraham far away, and Lazarus by his side. So he calls out, "Please, Father Abraham, take pity on me. Send Lazarus to give me a drink of cool water, just a brief respite from this raging inferno."

'But Abraham says, "And what concern did you show Lazarus during your earthly life? You barely spared him a thought. In any case, a chasm lies between this place and yours, so no one can cross between them."

'The rich man then says, "If you can't help me, please send Lazarus back to earth to warn my five brothers, so that they can avoid my fate."

'"They already have plenty of warnings in the Scriptures," replies Abraham.

'"Yes," says the rich man, "but they'll be convinced if they see a dead man come back to life!"

'"Oh no they wouldn't," said Abraham. "If they don't take the Scriptures seriously, they won't believe even if someone defeats death."'

Jesus teaches more about forgiveness

Jesus told his followers, 'Temptation is inevitable in this life, but people who cause others to sin would be better off dead! Watch one another's backs. If your fellow believers sin, point it out. If they repent, forgive them. Even if they sin repeatedly, you must forgive them if they repent.'

His followers were dismayed. 'We don't have enough faith for this!' they said.

'You only need a tiny amount of faith,' Jesus told them. 'Just a mustard seed of faith would enable you to remove a tree and plant it in the sea!

'Imagine a farmer has a servant working in the fields. When the servant finishes his day's work, does he go straight to his own supper? Of course not. He has to serve the farmer his dinner first, and only after that can he enjoy his own meal. And does the farmer thank the servant for doing what is, after all, his duty? Your attitude should be the same: "Whatever we did, we were only doing our duty."'

'Temptation is inevitable in this life'

Jesus heals ten lepers

On his way to Jerusalem, Jesus entered one village on the border between Galilee and Samaria. Ten lepers came out to meet him. They stood at a respectful distance and called, 'Have pity on us.'

'Go and let the Jewish priests examine you,' Jesus instructed them. While they were on their way, they were healed.

One of them hurried back to Jesus, shouting out his thanks to God. He fell to his knees before Jesus and thanked him too. He was a Samaritan.

'What happened to the others?' asked Jesus. 'All were healed, yet only one – a foreigner! – has come back to give thanks to God. Come on, up you get. Go on your way. Your faith has healed you.'

Jesus explains about the coming of God's Kingdom

Some of the religious leaders asked Jesus how they could identify God's Kingdom when it came. 'It doesn't work like that,' replied Jesus. 'It's not the dramatic event you're looking for. The Kingdom is already taking root within individuals and is seen in transformed lives.'

Then he said to his followers, 'There'll come a time when you look back longingly on the days when I was with you. *'When I return, there'll be no missing me!'* Oh, people will tell you they've seen me in this place or that. Ignore them! When I return, there'll be no missing me! My second coming will be as obvious as a flash of lightning against a night sky. But none of this can happen until I've been rejected and killed.

'The last days of earth will be like the days of Noah: people getting on with their lives, with no sense of impending doom. When the flood came, it took them all by surprise. You remember the story of Sodom and Gomorrah? Exactly the same thing happened. No one saw disaster coming until it struck.

'It will be the same when I return. No one will have any idea it's about to happen. When it does, don't hesitate for a moment. Don't look back. If you try to cling to life, you'll lose it – but entrust it to me, and you'll find it kept safe for you. When I return, people will be separated from one another in a moment.'

Jesus teaches his followers about persistence in prayer

Jesus told his followers this story to illustrate the importance of persistence in prayer. 'Imagine a judge, a really tough nut, who cares neither for God nor for justice. In the same town lives a woman who continually pursues him, asking him to award her justice against an enemy. Time and again, he refuses. But does she give up? No, she keeps asking and, after a while, she wears him down and he decides to help her just to stop her constant appeals.

'If that's the way that a flawed human judge responds, how much more will your heavenly Father answer your prayers? Prayer isn't a question of overcoming God's reluctance, but of laying hold of his willingness to help.

'However, when I return to earth a second time, will there be anyone with faith left to greet me?'

The story of the Pharisee and the tax collector

Jesus knew that some of his listeners thought very highly of themselves and looked down their noses at everyone else, so he told them this story. 'Imagine a religious expert and a tax collector. They both go to the temple to say their prayers. The so-called religious expert stands where everyone can see him and makes himself the focus of his prayers. *"Oh God, have mercy on me, a sinner"* "Oh God, thank you for making me a cut above other people – people like that grubby little tax collector over there. You will bear in mind, won't you, that I go without food twice a week? I'm particularly proud of that. And don't forget I give away ten per cent of my earnings."

'The tax collector, meanwhile, just stands in a corner, his face downcast. Striking his chest, all he says, over and over, is, "Oh God, have mercy on me, a sinner."

'I tell you, it's the tax collector who goes home at peace with God. God's ears are deaf to self-righteous prayers. Those who build themselves up will be demolished, while those who make no great claims for themselves will be given places of honour in God's Kingdom.'

Jesus is asked about divorce

The Pharisees tried to trick Jesus by asking him, 'What's your view on divorce? We believe any fault a husband finds in his wife gives him the right to get rid of her. What do you think?'

'Surely you know the Scriptures?' replied Jesus. '"In the beginning," we read, "God made human beings, male and female … And so the timeless pattern of human relationship was established. Generation after generation, men and women leave their childhood homes, commit themselves to one another, and become one." How can you separate what is no longer two but one?'

'But Moses allowed divorce,' they retorted.

'The Law recognises the brokenness of the human condition and addresses the hardness of human hearts,' Jesus explained. *'Don't belittle being single'* 'But divorce was never in God's original plan for man and woman and could never be his ideal. In fact, the only grounds for divorce are if one partner is unfaithful to the other.'

His followers said, 'If you're right, we're better off not marrying at all!'

'Don't belittle being single,' Jesus said. 'It's not for everyone, of course, and for some it's not what they would choose. But some are so focused on working for my Father's Kingdom that they decide not to get married.'

Jesus welcomes children

People loved to bring their children to Jesus, to ask his blessing on them.

One day, his followers tried to stop this happening, which made Jesus angry. 'Don't do anything to prevent these children coming to me. Their childlike faith and trust are the key to entering God's Kingdom. In fact, unless you're willing to trust as simply and deeply as they do, you'll stand no chance of getting in.' With that, he swept the children up in his arms and blessed them.

Jesus meets a rich young man

As Jesus got up to leave, a rich young man approached him. 'How can I get this eternal life you're talking about?' he asked.

'You know The Ten Commandments off by heart, I'm sure,' said Jesus.

'I've never broken one in my life,' replied the young man proudly. 'What more can I do?'

Looking into the man's eyes, Jesus' heart went out to him. 'There's just one thing,' he said. 'Your love of money is holding you back from truly following God. Sell everything you own and give the money to the poor. Then come and follow me. You'll gain far more than you lose, because there's more treasure in heaven than you could ever amass on earth.'

The man's face fell. Slowly, he turned and walked away. How he loved his wealth!

Seeing his expression, Jesus sighed. 'Being wedded to

wealth makes it hard to enter God's Kingdom,' he said. 'In fact, it would be easier to thread a needle with a camel!'

His followers, who had been brought up to believe that wealth was a sign of God's favour, were astonished to hear this. 'How on earth can anyone be saved, then?' they asked. 'You make it sound as though no one has a hope of entering God's Kingdom.'

'In a way,' said Jesus, 'you're right. It's impossible to achieve salvation through your own efforts, and *'What's in it for us?'* not even the richest person can buy their way in. But thankfully God loves to make the impossible happen, and he loves to welcome people into his Kingdom.'

'We've given up everything to follow you,' said Peter. 'What's in it for us?'

'When my Father straightens this world out,' Jesus replied, 'you will help me rule it and the rewards of eternal life will more than compensate for the cost of following me. All the sacrifices you've made will be worthwhile. That's a promise.

'Just remember, though, that the Kingdom's values are not those of this world. Those who push to the front of the crowd will find themselves at the back of the queue, while those who gladly accept a lowly place here will be the guests of honour in the Kingdom of God.'

The story of the workers in the vineyard

Jesus told another of his stories about God's Kingdom. 'Imagine a vineyard owner who needs labourers to work in it for the day. First thing in the morning, he goes out and hires some workers, promising to pay them at the end of the day. Throughout the day, he hires extra workers as he finds them, right up to the last moment. At the end of the day, the workers line up for their wages *First and last have* and the owner pays them all the same, *little meaning in* no matter how many hours they've *the Kingdom* worked. The ones hired at dawn are furious, but he tells them not to complain, as he's giving them exactly what he promised. They agreed to work for that amount. The owner has every right to be generous to those who came in late if he so wishes. God's Kingdom is like that. No one can claim to be better than anyone else just because they've been in it longer. First and last have little meaning in the Kingdom.'

Jesus again predicts his death

Those travelling with Jesus felt a mixture of anticipation and fear as they neared Jerusalem. Once more, he took the twelve aside and told them what to expect when they reached the capital. 'We'll soon be in Jerusalem, where all the ancient prophecies about me will come true. I will be betrayed and handed over to the religious rulers. They will condemn me and in turn hand me over to the Romans, who will mock, flog and then execute me. Three days later, I will rise from the dead.'

But his followers couldn't take in what he was saying.

Jesus teaches his followers about the nature of God's Kingdom

Convinced that Jesus was talking about an earthly kingdom, the mother of James and John took them to see Jesus. 'I want you to do something for me,' she smiled. 'Promise me you'll give my boys the best places in your kingdom.'

'You and your sons have no idea what you're asking,' Jesus told her. 'My Kingdom is like no other. You don't join it to further your own ambitions, but to serve others, even to the point of giving your life for them. Hand on heart, can you truly claim you're ready to drink this bitter cup of suffering with me?'

'Your thinking needs to change'

'Of course we are,' they replied.

'You don't have a clue what that means,' Jesus told them, 'but I'm afraid that you will, very soon. As for your request, I'm not responsible for the seating plan in God's Kingdom. The places you have requested are already reserved.'

Jesus' other followers were livid with James and John when they learned about this, and an argument broke out between them.

So Jesus called them all together. 'Your thinking needs to change. People tend to see leadership as an excuse to lord it over others and look after number one. But in God's Kingdom, you lead by serving others. Take a leaf out of my book. I didn't come in search of servants, but to find people I could serve. In fact, I'm about to lay down my life to save those who are lost.'

Jesus meets Zacchaeus the tax collector

As Jesus made his way through Jericho, a man named Zacchaeus joined the crowd. He was one of the chief tax collectors and had made a fortune fleecing his fellow Jews. He was eager to see Jesus, but couldn't see over the heads in front as he was quite short. So he got ahead of the crowd, climbed a tree and sat there, waiting for Jesus to walk by underneath.

When Jesus reached that very spot, he stopped. 'Hello, Zacchaeus,' he said. 'I've been expecting you. Come down. I'm staying at your house today.'

Zacchaeus couldn't get down quickly enough!

Seeing Jesus going to his house, the crowd were not pleased – Zacchaeus was not a popular man. 'Why would Jesus choose him?' they grumbled.

But Zacchaeus was no longer the same man they had come to loathe. 'Lord,' he said to Jesus, 'I'm giving away half of all I own to the poor. And those I've cheated, I promise to pay back four times over.'

Jesus looked him in the eye. 'Today salvation has come to this man's house. I came to find the lost and bring them home.'

Jesus heals a blind man

The road out of Jericho took them past the beggars outside the gate, including a blind man called Bartimaeus. When he learned that Jesus was going by, he shouted out, 'Jesus, Son of the great King, have mercy on me!' Those at the front of the crowd tried to hush him up, but that only made him shout all the louder.

Jesus stopped and called him over. 'What do you want me to do for you?' he asked.

'I want to see,' the man said.

'Your sight is restored,' Jesus said. 'Your faith has healed you.'

Instantly, Bartimaeus could see clearly and he followed Jesus, shouting out his thanks to God. As the crowd realised what had happened, they joined in.

Two other blind men followed him as he left the city. 'Take pity on us, Son of the Great King David,' they called out. He led them somewhere quiet and asked, 'Do you really believe I can restore your sight?'

'We do, Lord,' they replied.

Touching their eyes, Jesus said, 'What you believe can be done is done.' Instantly, their sight was restored.

Jesus enters Jerusalem riding a donkey

Coming over the Mount of Olives, Jesus saw Jerusalem spread out below him. Here he paused and sent two of his followers into the next village, with instructions to bring back a donkey no one had ridden before.

'The donkey will have a colt with her. Bring them both to me,' he told them. 'If you're challenged, simply say that the Saviour needs them and will return them to the owner shortly. No one will stop you.' Jesus did this to fulfil another ancient promise:

> *Tell Jerusalem to watch out for her King.*
> *When he comes, he'll be riding a donkey with its foal.*

His followers did as they were instructed and brought the donkey to Jesus. Fashioning a makeshift saddle with their cloaks, they helped Jesus on and started on their way.

There was a carnival atmosphere among his followers and crowds lined the road into the city. Some threw down their cloaks in front of him, while others cut down palm branches from nearby trees.

A single shout rose from the crowd as their excitement grew and they began to wonder what would happen when Jesus entered Jerusalem. 'Hosanna!' they cried, which means "save us". 'Hosanna to the great King, who comes in the name of the Lord! Bring back the glory days of King David!'

In next to no time, the whole city was buzzing with the news that Jesus was on his way and the shout grew even louder, as word went round that he was coming as a king.

Some of the Pharisees demanded that Jesus tell his followers to stop. 'That wouldn't do any good,' cried Jesus. 'If they don't shout, the very stones along the road will!'

As they drew nearer to Jerusalem, Jesus began to weep for its people. 'If only you could see what's just over the horizon. You can't see that I'm your Saviour and you're equally blind to the total destruction that will shortly overtake this city. Not one stone will be left on another when the assault comes.'

Jesus didn't stay in the city long that first day. He went into the temple, taking careful note of all he saw there, and then left to spend the night in a nearby village called Bethany.

Early the next morning, on the way back into Jerusalem, Jesus stopped by a fig tree, hoping to find some fruit to eat. Finding only leaves, he spoke to the tree: 'You'll never produce fruit again.'

Jesus drives traders from the temple

In Jerusalem, Jesus returned to the outer courtyard of the temple. He found it full of traders making a fortune out of those who came to worship. Some were charging exorbitant rates to change money, while others demanded huge prices for the small birds which the poor were allowed to offer in the temple sacrifices. It was pandemonium.

'Trust in God, and the impossible becomes possible'

Jesus began to throw out the traders, overturning their tables and scattering their coins everywhere. He blocked those trying to bring in things to sell, shouting, 'Our holy writings say that this temple is to be a place of prayer, not of profit! God made it a place of sanctuary, but you've turned it into a den of thieves!'

People flocked to Jesus at the temple and he healed those who were sick or disabled. Children ran around, shouting, 'Hosanna! Praise the Son of the Great King!'

This drove the religious authorities to distraction and hardened their resolve to find a way to dispose of Jesus permanently. What they feared most of all was the loss of their own power, which they could feel waning day by day.

'Do you hear what these children are saying? Stop them!' they demanded.

'Of course I can hear them,' replied Jesus. 'And why stop them? This was predicted long ago:

'The Saviour will be greeted by the joyful shouts of children.'

Once again, as night fell, Jesus left the city for the nearby village of Bethany.

The next morning, Peter pointed out that the fig tree Jesus had cursed had withered right down to its roots.

'That's child's play,' said Jesus. 'Trust in God, and the impossible becomes possible. Only believe in his power, and you can move mountains. If you ask God for something, believe that he will answer. Just make sure you're not holding anything against anybody else. You must forgive everyone everything, so that God will forgive you.'

The opposition of the religious leaders intensifies

Each day, Jesus went to the temple to teach the people. Even though the religious authorities were determined to kill him, they couldn't work out how to do it without alienating the people, who hung on Jesus' every word.

One day, a group of religious experts confronted Jesus. 'What makes you think you have the right to behave like this?' they demanded. 'You have no authority at all!'

'I'll answer your question if you answer one of mine,' Jesus replied. 'Tell me about John the baptiser. Was his ministry divinely inspired or merely human?'

That stumped them and they withdrew to confer together. 'How should we answer?' they asked one another. 'If we say John's ministry came from God, he'll ask why we rejected it. But if we say it was merely human, the people will turn against us, as they all believe John was sent from God.'

'I'll answer your question if you answer one of mine'

So, rather lamely, they said, 'We don't know.'

'Well then,' said Jesus. 'If you can't work that out, there's not much point discussing the origin of my authority with you, is there?'

The story of the two sons

Jesus said, 'Imagine a father with two sons. One day, he asks the first to go and work in his vineyard. The son refuses, but later thinks better of it and off he goes. Meanwhile, the father has also asked the second son, who readily agrees, but then doesn't go. Which one did what the father wanted?

'You religious know-it-alls are just like the second son. You say all the right things, but when it comes to actually doing what God wants, you're not interested. Whereas the people you look down your noses at, those who don't fit your idea of what's right and proper, are flooding into God's Kingdom ahead of you, because they're willing to amend their lives to please him.'

The story of the wicked tenants

Jesus then told the people this story. 'Imagine a man who plants a vineyard. He spares neither expense nor effort to get it just the way he wants it, before renting it out to some local farmers. Come harvest time, the owner sends one of his servants to collect his portion of the crop.

'But the tenants beat him up and kick him out. Another servant goes, but is treated worse than the first. The third one is killed. Servant after servant tries to collect the owner's due. Some are beaten, others killed.

'Finally, the owner decides to send his own son. "Surely," he thinks, "they'll respect him." Far from it! They see the son coming and say to themselves, "Here comes the son and heir. If he disappears, there'll be nobody to inherit. Then what's to stop us keeping the vineyard for ourselves?" So they seize the son and kill him.

'What do you think the owner does about that? I'll tell you. He kills those wicked tenants and rents his vineyard out to others who will give him his share of the crop.'

'So they seize the son and kill him'

The people realised this was a story about the people of Israel and cried out, 'Surely this can never be?'

'Why then,' asked Jesus, 'do the ancient prophecies talk of a stone which the builders discard, yet which ends up as the keystone in the whole building?'

Looking straight at the religious leaders, he said, 'I'm sure you remember this ancient prophecy:

> *The stone rejected by the builders will become the keystone for the whole building.*

'You're like those wicked tenants in the story. God will take away his Kingdom from you and invite in those whose lives produce a harvest for him. I am that keystone, carefully chosen by the architect, which you so arrogantly refuse to recognise. Make sure you're not underneath when it falls.'

The religious leaders knew this story was told at their expense and looked for a way to arrest him. Only fear of the people stayed their hand, because the crowds revered Jesus as a prophet from God. So they stalked off.

The Pharisees try to trap Jesus

The Pharisees decided that their best hope of getting rid of Jesus was to trap him into saying something that would land him in hot water. So they got together with some of King Herod's supporters and began to flatter him, hoping to trip him up.

'What a great teacher you are!' they fawned. 'And so full of integrity. We admire the way you teach God's truth without fear or favour. So we're sure you'll have an opinion on whether we should pay taxes to the Romans?'

This was a real bone of contention in Jewish society, for Roman taxes were an ever-present reminder of the fact that their country was occupied. But Jesus spotted the trap and stepped round it. 'Toss me a coin,' he said. 'Now, whose image does it bear, and whose name is inscribed on it?'

It was a brilliant reply and left his opponents speechless

'The emperor's,' they replied.

'There's your answer, then,' said Jesus. 'If it belongs to Caesar, give it to him. Just make sure you don't do less when it comes to serving God.' It was a brilliant reply and left his opponents speechless, so they slipped away.

The Sadducees challenge Jesus about life after death

Now the Sadducees weighed in with their own question. Another faction within the ruling religious elite, they didn't believe in life after death.

'You know the Law of Moses,' they said. 'He decreed that if a man's brother dies without having children, the man must marry his brother's widow and have children by her, in order to preserve his brother's name. Imagine seven brothers. The first one marries, but dies childless. Each brother in turn marries the woman, but dies without giving her children. Last of all, she dies. Apart from being one very unhappy woman, whose wife will she be in the world to come?' They sat back smugly, believing this ridiculous tale had clinched the argument in their favour.

'What nonsense!' said Jesus. 'All this shows is how little you understand about your own holy writings or God's power. Marriage belongs to this age. It won't exist in eternity, any more than death will. All who enter eternal life will be God's children. But you're quite wrong about the world to come, and I can prove it from the very writings you revere. Moses himself refers to God as the God of Abraham, Isaac and Jacob. Now, all three were long dead when Moses wrote that. You surely don't believe that God is the God of the dead, do you? No. Of course not! In which case, the only conclusion is that Abraham, Isaac and Jacob live on.'

Once again, the crowds were astonished to hear Jesus teach.

The Pharisees ask Jesus about the Commandments

Then the Pharisees resumed their attack, putting up one of their legal experts to question Jesus. 'Teacher,' he asked, 'tell us which of all the Commandments is the most important.'

'God's Law gives us two main principles by which to live,' Jesus replied. 'They govern our relationship with him and with one another. First, we are to remember that there is only one God. We are to love him totally, with every fibre of our being. Second, he calls us to love everyone else just as much as we love ourselves. Devote yourself to these two principles, which encompass the life of God's Kingdom, and you'll find that all God's other laws flow from these two.'

The way we live is far more important than any religious ritual'

'That is well said,' confessed the man, clearly impressed by the way Jesus had answered. 'The way we live is far more important than any religious ritual.'

'You couldn't give an answer like that without being close to God's Kingdom,' Jesus told him.

Jesus asks a question of his own

Jesus pressed his advantage with a question of his own. 'What do you believe about the promised Saviour? Who is his father?'

'King David, of course,' they replied.

'So how do you explain David's psalm in which he calls the Messiah "Lord"? How can the Messiah be his son?'

His opponents were stunned into silence and from that time on, no one had the nerve to question him any more.

Jesus warns against religious hypocrisy

Jesus then told the crowds and his own followers, 'Don't think I disregard tradition and authority. Your religious leaders can trace their authority right back to Moses, so you owe them respect. Just don't copy them, because they don't practise what they preach. They've added so many petty rules to God's original Law that they actually make it harder for people to live God's way. What they should be doing is lightening the load, but they don't lift a finger to help.

'Don't be fooled by their apparent piety. Everything they do is for show. They make sure to be seen in the right places and, of course, they expect the best seats, whether in the synagogue or at dinner parties. And above all, don't they just love to hear you call them "Teacher"…

'But it's all a sham. Behind the scenes, their lives are crooked and hypocritical. One moment they'll deprive a widow of her home, thinking they can make up for it the next minute with one of their flowery prayers which go on and on. They may think a lot of themselves and they may even get away with it here on earth, but what a day of reckoning they've got coming!

'That's not the way in God's Kingdom. God alone is your

Lord, your Master and your Teacher. You're all family, equal before him. Don't call anyone "Father" except God, or "Teacher" except me. The greatest among you will be the one who gladly serves the rest. If you don't puff yourself up on earth, you won't have to be deflated when you enter my Father's Kingdom.'

Turning back to the religious leaders, Jesus shouted, 'A plague on you for slamming the door of God's Kingdom in people's faces! You compound your own refusal to accept God's invitation by doing your best to stop anyone else getting in.

'You'll pull out all the stops to convert someone to your way of thinking, but then truss them up in all your man-made rigmarole and mumbo-jumbo.

'You fancy yourselves as spiritual guides, but you're as blind as bats. You come up with all sorts of rules which make no *'You rob God by turning a blind eye to injustice'* sense. You get all worked up about the little things, like giving a tenth of your goods to the temple, but you don't even notice the really important things. In fact, you rob God by turning a blind eye to injustice, by failing to show mercy. You're not trustworthy. You jump on other people for the most minor infringements of your rules, yet turn a blind eye to your own corruption and deceit.

'A plague on you! You diligently wash every last speck of dirt from your cups and plates, but your own inner lives reek with indulgence and greed. You need to pay more attention to your hearts than your crockery.

'You're like a pit of writhing snakes. How can you hope to get off scot free after all you've done? Even now God sends out good people to show you how to live, and you do away with them all. And now you're about to cap it all by killing his own Son. How do you think you'll escape God's judgement?'

Jesus notices a widow's generosity

Jesus sat for a while, watching people coming and going in the temple courts, putting money in the collection box. Rich people would carelessly toss in a wad of notes, keen for others to notice and admire them. But then Jesus spotted an old widow, poor as a church mouse, who quietly slipped in just a couple of coins.

'See that?' he asked his followers. 'She has just given the biggest gift of the day. The others hardly put a dent in their wallets, but she has given God all she had.'

Jesus outlines the future to his followers

Later, as they were leaving the temple, one of his followers began to rave about its beauty – what a magnificent building it was, the result of so many rich gifts over the years!

'Take a good look at it,' said Jesus, 'for a day will come when it will be little more than a pile of rubble.'

They left the city, walked up to the Mount of Olives and sat there, looking back across at the temple on the other side of the valley.

'When's all this going to happen?' they asked him. 'Will there be any warning? How will we know the world's about to end?'

Jesus said, 'Be on your guard against deception. Don't be fooled by anyone who claims to be me. Don't be taken in by people who specify times and dates for the end of the world. Don't let rumours of war rattle you. Wars and natural disasters are simply part of the fabric of this broken world, but they don't mean "the end is nigh". They're more like the first contractions of a woman going into labour.

'Be prepared for the worst. This world will not be an easy place in which to be my follower. The time will come when anyone who follows me will be hated, wherever they are. You'll be mocked and persecuted and even killed because of me, often by people who claim to be religious. *'Whatever happens, don't give up'* The authorities will try to make you give up your faith and some of you will even betray one another. They'll arrest you, hold show trials and parade you in public before politicians and world leaders. Don't worry about what you'll say. When the time comes, the Spirit of God himself will inspire you with just the right words. Although it will be grim for you, this is one way in which the good news about me will travel the world.

'False teachers will arise, claiming to bring messages from God, and will lead many astray. I'm afraid that even family members will betray one another. It will be hard to keep the flame of faith burning. But whatever happens, don't give up. If you stand firm through it all, you'll be saved in the end.

'The end can't come until all this has happened. A time of unimaginable distress lies ahead. Watch out for armies coming to lay siege to Jerusalem. Remember the ancient prophecies:

our holiest places will be defiled in an act of desecration
so abominable it will be unmistakeable.

'As soon as you catch wind of this, get out of the city as quick as you can. Don't look back. Don't stop for anything: run for your lives! What a terrible time it will be, especially *'My return will be like* for expectant mothers and those *lightning against the* with young children. Don't think *darkness of night'* the attackers will spare women and children. They'll kill and enslave without compunction. Jerusalem herself will be laid waste. Pray it doesn't happen in winter.

'The turmoil of those days will be worse than anything the world has ever known, or will ever know again. God will limit that time for your sake, or no one would survive.

'Don't forget, if anyone tells you I've come back, don't believe them for a moment. Plenty of false "messiahs" and gurus will appear before the end. Some will even pull off miracles in their attempts to deceive you. Close your ears to their claims. I'm warning you now so that you won't be taken in. When I come back, you won't need to be told. My return will be like lightning against the darkness of night: you won't miss it.'

Jesus teaches his followers about his own return

'After that, everyone on earth will be terrified by extraordinary events in the skies, just as the prophets said. The sun will grow dim, the moon will fail, planets and stars will be shaken from their places and freak storms will lash the earth, causing widespread panic.

'And that's when everyone alive will see me, riding the clouds as I return to earth in power and splendour. With a blast of trumpets, God's angels will gather all my followers from the four corners of the earth. People will run for cover, but you'll have no need to hide. Stand tall, lift your faces, drink it all in, savour the imminent arrival of your final salvation.

'So watch out and learn to read the signs in the same way that you read the seasons. You see a tree begin to blossom and you know that summer is just around the corner.

'So, when you see these things, you will know that the Kingdom is on its way. The human story won't end until all this happens. So keep hold of everything I've taught you. Heaven and earth will end, but my words will stand for ever.

'Don't waste time trying to guess precisely when I'm about to return. Not even I know the date and time my Father has set. Remember Noah and his ark? No one else seemed to notice, they just carried on life as usual, oblivious of what was coming, until without warning the flood swept them away. My return will be as dramatic as that. Two people will be standing together, and the next moment one will be gone.'

Stories about faithfulness

'I'm looking for those I can trust, like a king who leaves his servants in charge of his property while he's away, each with a specific task. When the king returns, he expects to find the servants doing exactly as they have been instructed and ready to hand back the keys of the house. Faithful servants will be well rewarded.

'But what if the servants should think to themselves, "The old boy won't be back for ages," and begin to act as if they owned the place? What if they invite all their friends in for a wild party, working through the king's food and wine like there's no tomorrow, only for the king to return unexpectedly, finding his home in uproar? I dread to imagine what he will do! So then, live as my faithful servants, expecting my return every day. Don't nod off, because I could come at any time of day or night. Make sure I don't find you fast asleep.

'Or imagine a group of servants waiting for their master to return from a wedding reception. They have no way of knowing exactly when he's coming back, but they know he'll want them ready to open the door the moment he does. It could be the middle of the night before he comes home. The only way those servants can be sure to be ready is to wait up for him. They daren't slip

'Live as my faithful servants, expecting my return every day'

off to bed for a few hours, hoping not to be caught out. When he comes home and finds his servants ready to greet him, he'll reward them for their faithfulness.

'Imagine a man who has been tipped off that a thief is planning to break into his house that night. He's going to be on his guard, isn't he? No way will the thief be able to take him by surprise then. So you must be constantly vigilant, waiting for my return. It could come at any time.

'Imagine a wealthy man who has a number of businesses. He appoints a manager for one of them and expects him to run the company well in his absence. If the manager steps up to the mark and does a good job, he'll be given much more responsibility. But if he abuses his position, thinking he can take things easy, neglect his duties and bully the employees, he's going to find himself out on his ear, with no job and no future prospects.

'Any servant who knows what's required but won't do it can expect to be punished more severely than one who didn't know what his master wanted. The more you have been given, the greater your responsibility for what you do with it.

'Guard your hearts as a farmer does his fields, making sure that no weeds creep in. Some people will fall into despair, or abandon themselves to drunkenness and other pleasures which leave them empty. For them, my return will be like a trap springing shut. So be on your guard and make prayer a constant habit, so that you're prepared and ready to face me whenever I come back.'

The story of the bridesmaids

Jesus said, 'Imagine a group of bridesmaids whose job it is to light the way for the bridegroom. But half of them haven't bothered to make sure they have spare oil for their lamps. Something delays the bridegroom and they all fall asleep.

'Then, as midnight chimes, they're woken by voices. "Here he comes! He's on his way. Get ready to greet him." Those who weren't prepared can't get their lamps to light. "Please," they beg the others, "give us some of your oil."

'"You must be joking," the others reply. "We don't have enough for us all. You'll have to go and buy some more." But *"Please," they beg the others, "give us some of your oil"* while they're on their way to the shops, the bridegroom arrives and the party begins. When the other bridesmaids come back, it's too late and they find themselves locked out. How foolish they were! Watch out that the same thing doesn't happen to you when I return.'

The story of the king and his servants

Jesus knew that people had all sorts of misconceptions about God's Kingdom and how it would appear, so he told them this story.

'Imagine a prince who has just learned that he is to be king. He has to travel to his coronation and has to leave his estate in the hands of his three servants. So he calls them together and gives each a sum of money depending on their abilities. "See what you can do with this while I'm away," he tells them. The first two decide to invest what they have been given and each doubles the original sum. But the third simply stashes it under his mattress.

'When the king returns, he summons his servants and asks what they have done with the money. The first two report that they have made handsome profits and the king is delighted. "Excellent," he says to both of them. "Well done! I'm fortunate to have such loyal and faithful people working for me. This will mean promotion for you: I'm putting you in charge of some of the cities I now rule as king."

'The third comes in with some cock-and-bull story about his lord being harsh and unjust and says he was too scared to risk doing anything at all. "But I've kept what you gave me. Here it is, safe and sound."

'"Well," says the king. "We'll let your own words be your judge. So that's what you think you know about me, is it? Yet these other servants weren't afraid to take risks. They seem to know me rather better than you do! They know I'm someone they can trust. At the very least you should have put my money in the bank, where it would have earned a good rate of interest while I was away. Instead, you've blown it: you're fired."

'Turning to his other servants, he orders, "Take his money away from him and give it to the first servant. To those who have trust in me, more will be given. But from those who have no trust in me, everything will be taken away."'

Jesus warns that judgement will come one day

Jesus said, 'When I return as King, I'll summon every human to appear before my judgement throne and settle accounts with me. I'll separate everyone into two groups.

'To the one group, I'll say, "My Father welcomes you into his Kingdom. Your places have been kept for you since before the world began. When I lacked food, drink or clothing, you met my needs. You *"When I lacked food, drink or clothing, you met my needs"* offered me hospitality when all others turned their backs, and you even visited me in prison."

'"What are you talking about?" they'll ask. "When did we do any of these things?"

'"You weren't aware of it," I'll reply. "But you demonstrated your love for me by looking after your fellow believers whenever they were in need."

'To the other group, I'll have to say, "You're not welcome here. You'll share the fate of all those who rebel against me and spend eternity barred from my presence. When I lacked food, drink or clothing, you ignored my needs. You refused me hospitality, and you never visited me in prison."

'"What are you talking about?" they'll ask. "When did we fail to do these things?"

"You weren't aware of it," I'll reply. "But you showed your disregard for me by turning a blind eye to the needs of my followers. When you shunned them, you were shunning me."

'On that Day, humanity will be divided. Some will enter my Father's Kingdom and enjoy eternal life. Others will be left out in the cold.'

The Jewish chief priests conspire to kill Jesus

In the middle of the week, Jesus told his followers, 'The Passover festival is just two days away. That's when I'll be crucified.' This festival celebrates the Great Deliverance of the Jews from slavery in Egypt, when Moses led them to freedom.

The religious authorities, intent on killing Jesus, were still racking their brains to come up with some means of having him arrested. They met together in the palace of Caiaphas the Jewish high priest to go over their plan. 'Let's avoid the feast itself,' they said, 'or there'll be a riot.'

A woman anoints Jesus

One evening, Jesus was invited to dinner by a Pharisee named Simon. In those days, people leaned at a low table to eat, with their legs and feet stretched out behind them. A local woman, notorious throughout the town for the life she lived, learned that Jesus was there. During the meal she came in, bringing an alabaster jar of expensive perfume. *'What a shocking waste!'* Standing directly behind Jesus, she began to weep so that her tears fell on his feet. She then knelt and wiped away her tears with her own hair and kissed his feet. Then she broke the jar and poured its contents over his head and feet.

The other guests, including Jesus' followers, began to mutter under their breath. 'What a shocking waste! Think of all the good she could have done with that sort of money. She should have sold it and given the money to the poor instead.' They began to speak harshly to her.

Simon was thinking, 'This Jesus can't be from God if he lets this type of riff-raff defile him.'

'Let her be,' said Jesus. 'Why are you all attacking her? You've no idea what this means to me. The state of the world means you can spend the rest of your lives helping the poor. But this woman knows I don't have long to live and so she has come here to prepare me for the grave. Wherever the good news of God's Kingdom is told, she'll be remembered for this.'

Turning to Simon, Jesus said, 'I have a question for you. Imagine two men, both in debt to a local loan shark. One owes five hundred, the other fifty. Neither can repay their debt, so guess what? He cancels both their debts. Now, which of the debtors will be the most grateful?'

Simon answered cautiously, 'Well, I suppose it must be the one who was released from the biggest debt?'

'Spot on, Simon,' replied Jesus. 'You see this woman? When I arrived for dinner, you ignored all the normal acts of hospitality and welcome. You didn't even offer me water to wash my feet. She used her own tears. You gave me no kiss of welcome. She has covered my feet with kisses. Where was the oil from my host to anoint my head for dinner? A stranger, not even one of the other guests, has provided it out of her own pocket, so great is her sense of gratitude for all God has done for her! So I tell you, no matter *'She has covered* how colourful her past, no matter how *my feet with kisses'* poor her reputation, from this moment all her sins have been wiped clean – just as she wiped away her tears from my feet. Sadly, it's very hard for anyone who thinks they have no need of forgiveness to feel grateful.'

The guests, who had been watching this exchange, began to murmur amongst themselves. 'Who does he think he is to tell people their sins are forgiven?'

Turning to the woman, Jesus said, 'Your faith has saved you. Go in peace.'

Judas agrees to betray Jesus

For Judas, one of the inner circle of twelve, this was the final straw. God's Enemy had been worming his way into his mind for some time, and now he went to the authorities and told them he was ready to betray Jesus. They couldn't believe their luck and promised to pay him handsomely. He settled for thirty pieces of silver. From that moment, Judas bided his time, waiting for his opportunity.

Jesus spends his final evening with his friends

On the first day of the Passover celebration, Jesus sent Peter and John into Jerusalem to finalise preparations for their meal together. 'You'll see a servant carrying water to a house,' he said. 'Follow him and tell the owner that I need to use his house to celebrate Passover with my friends. He'll show you a large furnished room ready for us.' They went off and found it just as Jesus had told them.

That evening, as he was eating with his twelve closest followers, Jesus said, 'I've been looking forward to this moment for a long time. It will be the last time I share a Passover meal or drink wine again until my death and resurrection have ushered in the Kingdom of God.'

Then he dropped a bombshell. 'One of you here is going to betray me,' he told them. 'I must follow the path laid out for me, but the one who betrays me is heading for disaster. It would be better for him never to have been born.'

His followers were horrified and each one in turn protested his innocence. 'Surely you don't mean me?'

Even Judas had the nerve to ask whether he was the one. Jesus said simply, 'Yes, you are.'

That led to bickering about which of them was the most important. Jesus said, 'Things in God's Kingdom are upside down. In this world, leaders and rulers ride roughshod over *'My blood will be* people and claim it's for their own *poured out like wine'* good. But in God's Kingdom, the most important person is the one who serves everyone else. Who is more important in this world, the hotel guest or the waiter? The guest, of course! Follow my example and serve one another.

'You have stood by me, so I'm making you citizens of God's Kingdom, where you will feast to your hearts' content and also help me judge the people.'

Then he took a piece of bread and gave thanks to God. As he broke it and shared the pieces among his followers, he said, 'This is my body which will be broken for you, just like this. Eat it to remember me.'

Then he passed around the cup of wine, again giving thanks to God. 'My blood will be poured out like wine, sealing God's unbreakable promise to all who trust him. My blood will be shed for many so that all wrongdoing may be forgiven.'

Then he said to them all, 'The last time I sent you out on a mission, I told you not to take anything with you. But now, bring anything to hand. It's almost time. The ancient prophecies predicted that I would be counted a criminal and you'll see it happen with your own eyes.'

His followers replied, 'We've got a couple of swords.'

'More than enough,' said Jesus.

They sang a hymn together and went out into the night. Jesus led them to the Mount of Olives, a hillside outside the city. 'This very night,' he warned them, 'you're all going to desert me, fulfilling the ancient prophecy:

I will kill the shepherd and scatter his flock.

'But when I rise from the dead, I'll see you in Galilee.'

'You can count on me,' said Peter. 'No matter what the others do, I'll never abandon you.'

'Oh, Peter, Peter,' Jesus sighed, 'how little you know yourself! The Enemy has you in his sights and will do everything to break you. I'm praying that your faith will bring you through. When you're back on course, strengthen the others.'

Peter said, 'I'm ready for anything, even if it means prison or death.'

'Peter, Peter,' said Jesus again. 'Before the first cock crows tomorrow, you will deny all knowledge of me, not just once, but three times.'

'Never,' Peter swore. 'I'd sooner die than abandon you.' And they all said the same.

Jesus prays in the garden of Gethsemane

Leading them into a garden called Gethsemane, Jesus told his disciples, 'Wait here. I need to pray for a while.'

Taking Peter, James and John deeper into the garden, Jesus became visibly distressed and said to them, 'I don't know how I'm going to get through what lies ahead. The very thought of it crushes me. Don't leave me on my own. Stay and keep watch with me.'

He walked forward and, a few steps later, collapsed to the ground. 'Father,' he cried out, 'you can do anything. If there's any way out of this, please rescue me. But you know my deepest desire is to fulfil your purposes. I'm ready to do whatever you ask of me.'

When he returned to his three friends, he found them all asleep. Waking Peter, he demanded, 'Is one hour too much to ask? Stay awake and ask God for strength to resist the temptation you're going to face. I know your hearts are in the right place, but God's Kingdom won't be built on good intentions alone. Don't let your resolve weaken.'

Leaving them once more, Jesus continued to pray. 'Father,' he cried, 'if there's no other way, you know I'm ready to go through with it. I'm yours to command.'

When he had to wake his friends a second time, they were so ashamed that they could barely bring themselves to look at him. So he left them for a third time, continuing to pray fervently, asking his Father for escape, but promising his obedience whatever the outcome. An angel appeared to steel his nerve, yet he was so overwhelmed with distress that he began to sweat blood.

Jesus then woke his followers a final time. 'Are you still asleep? Well, you've had all the rest you're going to get. On your feet! The time has come. See? The traitor approaches.'

Jesus is betrayed and arrested

As he spoke, an armed mob sent by the religious authorities appeared, led by Judas, who walked straight up to Jesus and kissed him.

'No need for pretence, my friend,' said Jesus quietly. 'Just do what you've come to do.'

The kiss was the sign Judas had given the mob, and they seized Jesus.

'Am I a revolutionary all of a sudden?' asked Jesus. 'Or a disturber of the peace, that you come for me armed to the *'Violence leads to* teeth? Why not simply grab me in the *death, never life'* temple? I've been there day after day, right under your noses, and you haven't lifted a finger against me. Instead, you've waited for darkness to make your move.'

His followers began to panic and one struck out with his sword at a servant of the Jewish high priest, cutting off his ear.

'That's enough,' Jesus said and, reaching out his hand, he restored the ear as if the cut had never happened. 'Violence leads to death, never life. If I wanted to use force, I could summon battalions of angels to my side. But everything must take its course, just as it was written long ago.'

At this, Jesus' followers turned tail and ran, melting into the shadows. The mob got hold of one, but he managed to wriggle free of his robe and fled naked into the night.

The mob took Jesus to the home of the Jewish high priest, where the Jewish Council had gathered.

Peter followed in the shadows and managed to slip into the

courtyard of the house, where he joined a group of soldiers sitting round a fire.

The religious leaders couldn't find a single piece of evidence against Jesus. They weren't short of people who were willing to trot out trumped-up charges against him, but even they contradicted each other. The whole thing was a sham. Finally, two men did manage to get their stories to agree. 'He boasted about destroying the temple and then rebuilding it in three days!'

Peter denies being a follower of Jesus

Outside in the courtyard, one of the serving girls was staring at Peter. 'You're one of Jesus' followers, aren't you?' she said.

'I've no idea what you're talking about,' Peter said, loudly enough for them all to hear, and moved away.

Another girl recognised him. 'Look,' she said. 'He was with Jesus.'

'You've got it all wrong,' Peter swore. 'I've never even met the man!'

A little later, they all challenged Peter. 'Come off it,' they said. 'Your northern accent gives you away as one of Jesus' men.'

Peter began to swear and curse like a trooper. 'How many times do I have to tell you? I ... don't ... KNOW HIM!'

At that very moment, a cock's crow rang out in the chill of the new dawn. Peter remembered what Jesus had said. Running out of the courtyard, he broke down and wept uncontrollably.

Jesus is put on trial before the religious leaders

As dawn broke, Jesus was taken before the hastily convened court of Jewish leaders. Caiaphas the Jewish high priest rounded on him. 'What do you say to the charges against you?' he demanded. But Jesus remained silent, until Caiaphas asked him outright, 'Are you the Christ, the Son of God?'

They flew at Jesus, screaming, spitting and lashing out with their fists

'Yes, I am,' Jesus replied, 'and one day you will see me at God's right hand and returning to earth on the clouds.'

This was all Caiphas needed to hear. 'Blasphemy!' he shouted, tearing at his robes in a blind fury. 'What more proof do we need? He's guilty as charged.'

'His own words condemn him,' the others shouted. 'He must die!' They flew at Jesus, screaming, spitting and lashing out with their fists.

He was blindfolded and they began to beat him and mock him. 'Come on, Son of God!' they shouted. 'Surely you can tell which one of us is hitting you?'

Then the guards took him away and they too beat him.

Jesus appears before Pontius Pilate, the Roman governor

Having agreed that Jesus must die, the religious authorities handed him over to the Roman governor, a man called Pilate.

The Jewish priests reeled off the charges against him, but Jesus remained resolutely silent, much to Pilate's amazement. 'Do you hear what they're saying?' Pilate demanded. But Jesus said nothing.

'They tell me you claim to be king of the Jews,' he persisted.

'Yes, I am,' Jesus replied.

'I can't find anything against this man,' Pilate told the Jewish priests, but they continued to accuse him.

'He's guilty of treason … He's a rabble-rouser, encouraging people not to pay the Roman taxes … He's been whipping up the people all the way from Galilee!'

When Pilate heard that Jesus came from Galilee, he saw a way of avoiding the issue. Galilee was under the control of Herod, the empire's puppet king of that region. So Pilate ordered Jesus to be taken to him. Herod was delighted: he had wanted to see Jesus for some *'This man doesn't* time and hoped he would perform a *deserve to die'* miracle or two. But despite a barrage of questioning, accusation and abuse from the religious leaders, Jesus said not one word. Losing interest, Herod sent Jesus back to Pilate. The two rulers had been enemies, but from that day they became allies.

Pilate called all the religious leaders together and suggested a compromise. 'You have done your best to convince me that this man's a dangerous revolutionary, but I haven't been able to find anything against him. Obviously, neither has Herod, or he wouldn't have sent him straight back here. This man doesn't deserve to die. Why don't I just have him beaten and then let him go?'

But the religious leaders began to shout even more fiercely for Jesus to be put to death.

Three times Pilate tried to reason with them, but they drowned him out, shouting, 'Kill him! Kill him!'

Pilate was no fool. He could see the envy which lay behind the charges against Jesus. He had one more card to play, a popular Passover tradition he himself had established of allowing the festival crowds to choose one prisoner to be set free.

'Time to choose this year's prisoner,' he called out to the people. 'You can have Jesus, the one you call "Saviour", or Barabbas.' Barabbas was a real thug and Pilate was sure they would choose Jesus.

While the crowds were debating, Pilate received a note from his wife. 'I've had bad dreams about this man. Don't get mixed up with him. He's innocent.'

But the religious authorities whipped up the crowd to demand that Barabbas be released.

'Well?' Pilate demanded. 'Have you made your minds up?'

'Give us Barabbas!' they shouted.

'What about Jesus, then?' asked Pilate. 'What shall I do with him?'

'Kill him!' they bellowed.

'Why? What's his crime?' Pilate replied.

There was no persuading them. 'Crucify him!' they yelled, over and over again. Pilate hadn't become governor without recognising trouble when he saw it. He knew when to cut his losses and saw now that the only way to pacify the mob was to abandon Jesus to his fate. So he publicly washed his hands, in front of them all. 'I'm not responsible for what you do to this man,' he said.

'On our own heads be it,' the crowds shouted.

So Pilate had Jesus whipped and handed him over to his troops, who took Jesus into their guardroom, stripped off his clothes and dressed him in a scarlet robe. They twisted some thorn twigs together into a crude crown and stuck *'I've betrayed an innocent man'* it on his head. Kneeling in mock homage before him, they called out, 'Hail, man who would be king!' After beating him severely and covering him in spittle, they put his clothes back on him and led him away to be crucified.

When Judas realised that Jesus had been condemned to death, he was filled with remorse and tried to hand his blood money back to the Jewish priests. 'I've done a terrible wrong,' he said. 'I've betrayed an innocent man.'

'That's your problem,' they replied, refusing to take the money. 'It's nothing to do with us.'

So Judas flung the money at their feet, went outside and hanged himself.

The Jewish priests gathered up the coins. 'This money's tainted. We can't use it here.' So they bought a local potter's field, to be used as a graveyard for foreigners. It's still called 'Blood Acre' today. The prophet Jeremiah had predicted this long ago:

> *They put a price on his head, thirty pieces of silver,*
> *and with it bought the potter's field…*

Jesus is crucified

As they marched Jesus through the streets, the soldiers pulled a man out of the crowd and made him help Jesus carry his cross. His name was Simon and he was a visitor who had come to Jerusalem from Cyrene for the Passover celebration.

A large crowd followed, including many women who wept as they saw Jesus. Turning to them, he said, 'Don't cry for me, but for yourselves and your children. If the world can do this to me, there's no limit to its evil.'

'Father, forgive them, they don't know what they're doing'

Jesus was led to a place called 'Skull', where they offered him wine to deaden the pain, which he refused. As the soldiers stretched him out on the cross and drove nails through his feet and wrists, Jesus prayed, 'Father, forgive them, they don't know what they're doing.'

Lifting him up, they dropped the cross into its socket and then sat down to wait for him to die. As they waited, they played dice for his clothes.

It was about nine in the morning when they crucified Jesus between two thieves. The custom was to fix a notice above the victim's head detailing their crime. The one above Jesus read, 'The King of the Jews'.

The crowds who had come to see the killings taunted Jesus and shook their heads in scorn. 'Well, look at this! The big talker who was going to pull down our temple and rebuild it in three days has got his comeuppance!'

The Jewish priests joined in. 'Fancy yourself as our Saviour, do you? Hah! Looks like you can't even save yourself. If you really are the Son of God, prove it. Jump off that cross and then we'll believe in you!'

Even one of the criminals being crucified alongside him joined in the taunting and mockery. But the other one said, 'What's got into you? He might have been sentenced to death, but whereas we deserve what's happening, he has committed no crime.' Then he addressed Jesus. 'Don't forget me when you become king,' he pleaded.

Jesus looked at him and said, 'I give you my word. Today we'll be in paradise together.'

At around noon, the sun disappeared and an eerie darkness settled over the whole area. Three hours later, Jesus lifted his head and shouted out, 'Oh God, why? Why have you abandoned me?'

Some of the bystanders thought he had called out to Elijah. Someone stuck a sponge on a stick, soaked it with wine vinegar and raised it to Jesus' lips. Others said, 'Let him be. Let's see what happens.'

Then Jesus called out, 'Father, I entrust myself to your safekeeping.'

Jesus cried out once more, let out his final breath and died. The curtain blocking access to the most sacred part of the temple was torn in two and an earthquake shook the land. Tombs burst open and many holy people were raised from the dead. They went throughout the city and were seen by many witnesses.

'He must have been God's Son after all!'

Seeing all this, the centurion in charge of the execution party exclaimed, 'How could this man be guilty of any crime? He must have been God's Son after all!'

The crowds were filled with fear and scurried away. But Jesus' followers stood at a safe distance, forlornly watching everything that happened. They included the women who had followed him so faithfully all the way from Galilee.

Jesus is buried

One of the religious leaders was a rich man called Joseph. He was longing to see God's Kingdom come and hadn't supported the decision to have Jesus killed. A prominent member of the Jewish Council, he had secretly become a follower of Jesus and now saw an opportunity to play his part, however small.

Jesus had been executed on the day before the Day of Rest and Jewish Law therefore required that his body be buried before sunset. So Joseph went to Pilate and asked for permission to bury the body. Pilate was initially suspicious, wondering if this was a ploy to rescue Jesus before he died, so he double-checked with the soldiers who had crucified him. Satisfied that Jesus was truly dead, he agreed to Joseph's request.

So Joseph took the body, wrapped it in fresh linen and

placed it in his own tomb, which he sealed by placing a large stone over the entrance. Some of the women followed and noted where he had been laid to rest.

It was now Friday evening, so the women went home and prepared spices and oils to anoint the body – but they did nothing the next day, because it was the Day of Rest.

Pilate orders a guard on Jesus' tomb

The next day, the religious authorities sought audience with Pilate. 'Before he died, this conman put about the fantasy that he would rise again after three days,' they said. 'So will you have the tomb sealed and guarded, at least until tomorrow? Otherwise his followers might steal the body and claim that he has indeed come back to life. Imagine the trouble that could stir up.'

'Take some of my troops to stand guard duty,' said Pilate. 'Make that tomb as secure as a bank vault.'

So they sealed the stone at the mouth of the tomb and set a guard outside.

Jesus is seen alive

So it was on the first day of the week, the third day after Jesus was executed, that the women returned to the tomb, planning to tend to his body as custom required. Their only concern was that they wouldn't be able to roll the stone away from the entrance.

They went into the tomb and jumped with fright

When they arrived, however, they found the stone already moved, the guards sprawled on the ground as if dead and the tomb empty. They went into the tomb and jumped with fright at the sight of an angel, wearing a dazzling white robe.

'Don't be scared,' he said. 'I know why you're here. You're looking for Jesus, who was crucified, but you won't find him in a graveyard! He's alive, just as he promised. Look: you can see where his body lay. Go and tell the others that he'll be waiting for them in Galilee.'

As the women rushed off, they ran into Jesus himself. Falling to the ground, they clung to his feet and worshipped him.

'Don't be scared,' he said. 'Tell the others I'll see them back in Galilee.'

The women ran and told the men what they had seen and heard, but it didn't make sense to them. How could it be true?

Peter raced to the tomb and peered inside. Seeing only the pieces of linen lying on the floor, he walked away, trying to puzzle it all out.

Some of the guards went and reported what had happened. The religious leaders bribed the soldiers not to breathe a word of what had really occurred. 'Tell everyone this story,' they told them. 'Say, "His followers must have come while we were asleep and stolen the body." If Pilate gets wind of it, we'll square it all with him.'

So the soldiers pocketed the money and did as they were told – and their story is still doing the rounds today.

Jesus appears to two of his followers on the road to Emmaus

Later that day, two of Jesus' followers were returning home to their village, Emmaus, a few miles outside Jerusalem. As they mulled over everything that had happened in the last few days, Jesus joined them and walked along with them. They didn't realise it was him: who expects to see a dead man?

He asked them, 'What are you talking about?'

They were the very picture of dejection, all slumped shoulders and long faces. One of them, Cleopas, said, 'What planet have you been on these last few days? You must be about the only person alive who doesn't know what's been going on!'

'What has been going on?' asked Jesus innocently.

'They've killed Jesus of Nazareth, that's what! Oh, what a man – the things he said, the things he did! No one could have had the power he had unless God sent him. And what did our so-called religious leaders do *Jesus joined them* with him? Only handed him over to the *and walked along* Romans for crucifixion, that's what. And *with them* we'd pinned all our hopes on him. We really believed he was going to save the whole nation. The weird thing is, all this happened three days ago and now some of our women are telling stories of angels at his tomb and saying that he has risen from the dead! Some of the men went to check it out. They found the tomb empty, all right, but saw neither hide nor hair of him.'

Jesus said, 'Can't you put two and two together? It's all there in the ancient prophecies. God's prophets of old set it all down for you, detailing everything that would happen to the Messiah.' And he began to point out every reference in the Jewish texts which had been written about himself.

When they reached the outskirts of their village, Jesus made as if to carry on, but it was already dusk, so they persuaded him to stay with them. Once supper had been served, Jesus took some bread, gave thanks to God, broke it and began to hand it to them. At once, they knew who he was, but no sooner did they recognise him than he vanished. Turning to each other, they said, 'No wonder we felt so fired up as he talked to us on the road!'

Leaving their meal untouched, they set out to walk back to Jerusalem. Bursting into the room where Jesus' followers were gathered, they were just in time to hear that Jesus had appeared to Peter. So they added their own experience to the growing list of Jesus' appearances.

Jesus appears to his followers in Jerusalem

While they were swapping stories, Jesus suddenly appeared in the midst of them and said, 'Peace with you!' They were terrified, convinced he was a ghost. 'Don't be afraid,' said Jesus. 'Why did you doubt what I told you? See my hands and feet? Here are the holes left by the nails. It's really me! Touch me if you like. What ghost was ever made of flesh and bone?'

'What ghost was ever made of flesh and bone?'

Still they couldn't accept the truth, so he asked for some food and ate a piece of cooked fish before their very eyes.

Jesus appears to his eleven closest followers in Galilee

Jesus' eleven original followers went to Galilee as he had instructed them and found him there just as he had promised. They worshipped him, although some still held on to their doubts.

Jesus said, 'I've been given absolute authority. So now I commission you: go to the whole world, calling people everywhere to follow me. Baptise them in the name of the Father, the Son and the Holy Spirit and train them to obey my teaching. Don't worry. You'll never be alone again. I'll be with you every step of the way, to the very end of time.'

Jesus makes his final appearance and ascends to heaven

After spending some time with his followers in Galilee, Jesus sent them back to Jerusalem where he spoke to them one final time. 'Surely you remember all I taught you?' he said. 'Everything that has happened to me was carefully predicted in advance by God's prophets of old. I was always going to be put to death and I was always going to rise from the dead on the third day. It's all there in your holy writings – right under your noses!

'And now the good news of God's love and forgiveness for all who genuinely want a new start will flow out from Jerusalem to the four corners of the earth. You're my witnesses. Soon I will send you the power you need, just as God my Father has promised – but you must stay in the city until that time.'

He then took them out to Bethany. Lifting his hands in farewell and blessing, he was taken from their sight and they knew that he had returned to be with his Father in heaven. Now fully convinced that he was the promised Saviour, they returned to Jerusalem, their hearts bursting with joy. Day by day, they were to be found in the temple, praising God.

**To find out more about Christianity go to
christianity.org.uk**

Paul Langham

has been vicar of Christ Church Clifton, in Bristol, since
September 2010. He has also served as vicar of three churches
in Bath and as chaplain of St Catharine's College, Cambridge. He
is married to Jackie with whom he has four children, and is the
author of four Fresh Retelling Gospels as well as *Understanding
Revelation* (2005).

Bible Society
Trinity Business Centre
Stonehill Green, Westlea
Swindon SN5 7DG
biblesociety.org.uk
bibleresources.org.uk

ISBN: 978-0-564-04903-5
ISBN: 978-0-564-04913-4 (packs of 10)

Typesetting and production by Bible Society Resources Ltd, a wholly-owned
subsidiary of The British and Foreign Bible Society
Text design by Heather Knight
Original cover design of *Who?* by Patrick Knowles

BFBS/10M/2013
Printed and bound by CPI Group (UK) Ltd, Croydon, CR0 4YY